JULIAN H. GONZALEZ

Scotty Bowman added a ninth Cup to his collection, most among NHL coaches, passing mentor Toe Blake.

HANG IO

THE 'HANG 10' BOOK STAFF

Editor: Tom Panzenhagen

Designer: Christoph Fuhrmans

Photo editor: Diane Weiss

Photo technicians: Rose Ann McKean, Jessica Trevino, Kathryn Trudeau and Naheed Choudhry

Production editor: Bob Ellis

Assistant editor: Will McCahill

Copy editors: Alison Boyce Cotsonika, Bill Collison, Vince Ellis, Tim Marcinkoski, Carlos Monarrez, George Sipple, Shelly Solon

Project coordinator: Dave Robinson

Sports editor: Gene Myers

Director of photography: Nancy Andrews

Design and graphics director: Steve Dorsey

Special thanks: Laurie Delves, Carole Leigh Hutton, Ryan Huschka, Heath Meriwether, Rick Nease, Mitch Rogatz, Josh Szablewski, Martha Thierry, Mike Thompson

Dedicated to the memory of Robert G. McGruder.

Cover photo: Mandi Wright

Back cover photo: David P. Gilkey

Detroit Free Press

OTHER RECENT BOOKS BY THE FREE PRESS:

Time Frames
The Detroit Almanac
Ernie Harwell: Stories From
    My Life in Baseball
HeartSmart Kids Cookbook
State of Glory
Corner to Copa

The Corner
Century of Champions
PC@Home
Yaklennium
Believe!
Stanleytown

To order any of these titles, please call **800-245-5082** or go to **www.freep.com/bookstore**

A team for the ages

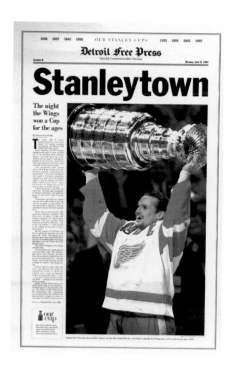

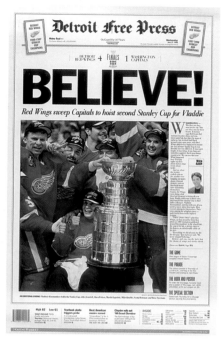

The gloves were tossed, the confetti came down, and into the happy heap they flew, the old guys and the new guys and the 41-year-olds and the 21-year-olds and the guys who just got a second or third championship and the guys who finally got their first. They leapt over the top. They barreled in from the side. Yzerman on top of Datsyuk on

MITCH ALBOM

top of Lidstrom on top of Hasek. Fedorov on top of Hull on top of Devereaux on top of Larionov. Old on new. Veteran on rookie. And in that delirious if somewhat toothless stack of players, the Detroit Red Wings evoked their team philosophy: In a pileup, everybody is a star.

And that's just the way they like it.

They came. They clicked. They conquered. The Greatest Hockey Roster Ever Assembled just finished the kind of season that leaves fans weeping with satisfaction. These Detroit players carried a dream from the opening night in October to the closing horn in June, when the final foe, the Carolina Hurricanes, was vanquished. And in all that time, not once did their dream exceed three colors: red, white — and silver.

The Cup Runneth Home.

Welcome back, Stanley.

"Everybody on this team at some point stepped up for a big play in a big game," said the joyous Captain, Steve Yzerman, after lifting the Stanley Cup, the most precious trophy in sports, for the third time. "The only thing that mattered was winning, and the only thing that mattered was the team."

And this, folks, was a team for the ages — and one that will never be the same because moments after the final horn, Scotty Bowman — who brought Detroit three championships in six years

— whispered in his owner's ear, "It's time to go."

He leaves on the highest of notes, having steered a veteran-heavy group that never faltered, never panicked and never seemed to tire. The Red Wings overcame the hottest team in hockey in the first round, a supposedly blistering goalie in the second, the defending NHL champions in the third, and the most dangerous kind of upstarts in the finals. Not one opponent resembled the other — except in the way they ended, skating off, shaking their heads, marveling at the tank that had just rolled over them.

They came. They clicked. They conquered.

"This is my dream come true," said Dominik Hasek, who had been the oldest Wing without a Cup. He turned to pour champagne on teammate Sergei Fedorov's head.

"Hey, look," Sergei laughed. "It's raining in Detroit."

Happy showers, everyone.

"There's no feeling like this,"

After 16 seasons of fruitless toil in the NHL vineyard, Luc Robitaille bloomed in the Wings' locker room. Steve Duchesne, lower right, found the trophy handy as a drinking vessel.

said an overwhelmed Luc Robitaille, wearing his first Stanley Cup champions' cap. "You work your whole life for this. . . . It was all worth it."

His children were there. All the Wings' children seemed to be there. And as their fathers skated around the ice with the Cup, they seemed to stitch the tapestry of this team's incredible season.

They came. The new additions. Hasek from Buffalo, Robitaille from Los Angeles, Brett Hull from Dallas, Fredrik Olausson from Sweden, Pavel Datsyuk from Russia. All arrived with a single goal — to reach the top of the heap by the end of the season.

They clicked. New players mixing with old. Young players learning from veterans. Czechs, Swedes, Canadians, Russians and Americans, leaving their egos at the door, dropping their superstar name tags, heeding the instructions of coaching legend Scotty Bowman and morphing under the quiet leadership of Steve Yzerman.

They conquered. Best record in hockey. Vancouver, St. Louis, Colorado and Carolina in the playoffs. If you knock out the rusty opening two games of the postseason, the Wings won four straight to advance, four of five to advance again, then six of their last seven to seal the deal. They didn't win every game. Just all the ones they had to.

The last came in Game 5, the season finale. The Wings had won three straight from Carolina and they picked up the beat like a needle being dropped in the middle of a jazz album. They outskated the Hurricanes. Outhustled them. Outquicked them. And finally outed them altogether.

Lord Stanley was back in Detroit for the third time in six years, and the 10th time in history.

We're a double-digit town now.

The Cup Runneth Home.

And then, the aftermath.

"It's time for me to go," said Bowman, 68, just minutes after the Wings' 3-1 victory and the on-ice ceremony. "I'm just so happy to be leaving with a winning team."

A team for the ages. If there was a single sports lesson in this team's success, it's that individual stardom is nowhere near as much fun as shared glory.

And there's no glory like Stanley coming home to papa. You could see that in the eyes of the three-time holders, like Yzerman, Fedorov, Kris Draper and Kirk Maltby, you could see it in the eyes of the second-timers like Hull and Chris Chelios — who waited 16 years between Cups — and you could see it most of all in the teary

eyes of the first-timers, like Robitaille and Hasek, who finally had been let into the secret society of their dreams.

You could see it in the jack-o'lantern smile of defenseman Steve Duchesne, 36 years old, a guy who has been on six teams and who never won a title and who took a puck in the mouth in Game 3 and lost a couple of teeth and was bleeding all over the place, yet only wanted to clean his shield and get back on the ice.

"I still got some lower ones left," he mumbled after that game.

And as long as there was a tooth to give. . . .

They came. They clicked. They conquered. There goes the Greatest Hockey Roster Ever Assembled. That happy heap, on which every player was a star, is forever the Red Wings' legacy, and it will not be forgotten, not around Detroit, not for a long, long time.

MANDI WRIGHT

Brendan Shanahan scored two goals, including the Stanley Cup winner, in Game 5. Afterward, he got an embrace from Scotty Bowman.

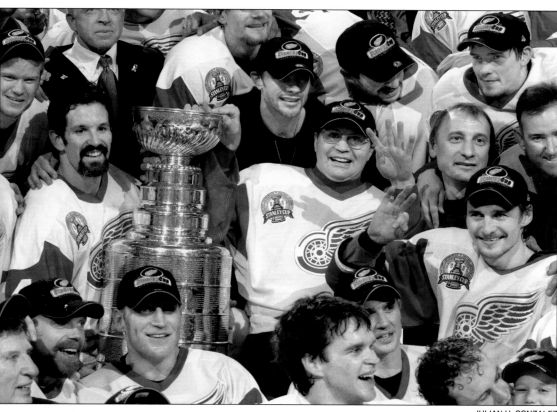

Vladimir Konstantinov had helped the Red Wings break their 42-year Cup drought in 1997, and he had inspired them in '98. They made him the center of the team photo in 2002.

JULIAN H. GONZALEZ

JULIAN H. GONZALEZ

The Tradition

DETROIT
RED WINGS

1935-36
STANLEY
CUP
CHAMPIONS

THE TEAM

COACH: Jack Adams (also manager).

HALL OF FAMERS (5): Adams, Marty Barry, Ebbie Goodfellow, Syd Howe, Herbie Lewis.

TOP PLAYERS: RW Larry Aurie (44 games, 16-18 – 34), C Barry (48 games, 21-19 –40), D Goodfellow * (48 games, 5-18 – 23), F Howe (48 games, 16-14 – 30), LW Lewis (45 games, 14-23 –37), D Bucko McDonald (47 games, 4-6 – 10, second in rookie of the year voting), LW John Sorrell (48 games, 13-15 –28).

GOALIE: Normie Smith (48 games, 24 wins, 6 shutouts, 2.04 goals-against average).

* Postseason All-Star.

THE SEASON

TEAM	W	L	T	PTS
Detroit	24	16	8	56
Mar'ns *	22	16	10	54
Toronto	23	19	6	52
Boston	22	20	6	50
Chicago	21	19	8	50
Rangers ^	19	17	12	50
Am'cans ^	16	25	7	39
C'diens *	11	26	11	33

*-Montreal; ^-New York

THE PLAYOFFS

ROUND ONE: Detroit eliminated Montreal Maroons, 3-0.

CUP FINALS: Detroit eliminated Toronto, 3-1.

THE FINALS

GAME 1: Detroit 3, Toronto 1.

GAME 2: Detroit 9, Toronto 4.

GAME 3: Toronto 4, Detroit 3 (OT).

GAME 4: Detroit 3, Toronto 2. Winning goal: Pete Kelly.

1935-36

DETROIT FREE PRESS FILE PHOTO

What a team! These Wings started a winning tradition — and quite possibly the tradition of drinking from the Cup.

Adams' boys down Leafs to bring Detroit its first Cup

April 11, 1936

BY DOC HOLST

TORONTO — The Red Wings Saturday night presented the City of Detroit with its first Stanley Cup after 10 years of bitter struggle in the National Hockey League.

They did it with a 3-to-2 triumph over the Toronto Maple Leafs, but not until after a crowd of 14,728 persons witnessed the Leafs put up another great last-period onslaught that once more almost saw them tie the score in the final minutes.

As in the game here Thursday night, it was a "goat" named Kelly that furnished the winning margin, but this time it was a redhaired Scotchman named Pete, a Kelly who works for a man named Jack Adams.

While it was young Kelly who made the final Wing goal to give them the one-point edge, two beautiful goals by a pair of veterans — Marty Barry and Ebbie Goodfellow — delivered the punch that sent the Leafs sagging toward eventual defeat.

It was Ebbie's goal in the second period that tied the score and started the men of Jack Adams on the way to the greatest honor to be won in hockey.

It was Barry's goal, 44 seconds later, that broke the tie and the Leafs' backs to give the Wings a lead which Toronto never was able to overcome.

The Stanley Cup was presented to Mr. James D. Norris, owner of the Red Wings, by (NHL) President Frank Calder at the Royal York Hotel immediately after the game.

President Calder informed Norris of the plan, and Norris said that was agreeable.

"Providing I can fill it with champagne and give all my players a drink," shouted the happy Norris.

1936-37

DETROIT FREE PRESS FILE PHOTO

The line of Larry Aurie, left, Marty Barry and Herbie Lewis put the Wings in line for their second straight championship.

THE TEAM
COACH: Jack Adams.
HALL OF FAMERS (5): Adams, Marty Barry, Ebbie Goodfellow, Syd Howe, Herbie Lewis.
TOP PLAYERS: RW Larry Aurie * (45 games, 23-20 – 43), C Barry * (47 games, 17-27 – 44, Lady Byng Trophy), D Goodfellow * (48 games, 9-16 – 25), F Howe (45 games, 17-10 – 27), D Bucko McDonald (47 games, 3-5 – 8).
GOALIE: Normie Smith * (48 games, 25 wins, 6 shutouts, 2.05 goals-against average, Vezina Trophy).
* Postseason All-Star.

THE SEASON

TEAM	W	L	T	PTS
Detroit	25	14	9	59
C'diens *	24	18	6	54
Boston	23	18	7	53
Mar'ns *	22	17	9	53
Toronto	22	21	5	49
Rangers ^	19	20	9	47
Chicago	14	27	7	35
Am'cans ^	15	29	4	34

*-Montreal; ^-New York

THE PLAYOFFS

ROUND ONE: Detroit eliminated Montreal Canadiens, 3-2.
CUP FINALS: Detroit eliminated N.Y. Rangers, 3-2.

THE FINALS

GAME 1: New York 5, Detroit 1.
GAME 2: Detroit 4, New York 2.
GAME 3: New York 1, Detroit 0.
GAME 4: Detroit 1, NewYork 0.
GAME 5: Detroit 3, New York 0. Winning goal: Marty Barry.

Red Wings first American team to repeat as Cup champs

April 15, 1937

BY DOC HOLST

A little country boy, Earl Robertson went to town last night.

Mr. Robertson became the outstanding hero of a hockey continent as he delivered his second shutout in a row to give the Detroit Red Wings a 3-to-0 victory over the New York Rangers as well as the precious Stanley Cup for the second time in a row.

It was the first time in the history of hockey that an American club had won the cup twice in a row. It was the first time that any club under the modern playoff system ever had won both the cup and the National Hockey League pennant twice in succession.

Marty Barry and Johnny Sorrell gave Detroit its winning goals with the aid of such stars as Hec Kilrea and Syd Howe, but calloused hockey fans expected those veteran gentlemen to be heroes. They never looked to Earl Robertson, the hobo of hockey, to come to the rescue of the most crippled team in hockey history and prove to even biased critics that the Red Wings of 1937 will stand alone when miracle teams are discussed.

Barry, the scoring hero of the last two games — and deservedly so — stood quietly in a corner pulling on his underwear and said:

"My goals wouldn't have been worth a damn without — "

Barry couldn't finish the sentence. He nodded over toward the bashful and flustered Robertson, pulling on his underwear also. ...

"There's the guy," Marty finally said. "Sorrell and I made the goals to win, but we won the Stanley Cup with him."

... After the game (coach) Jack Adams rushed across the ice, spoke over the radio, dashed back across the ice and had to be escorted by a dozen policemen before he could force his way into the Red Wing dressing room.

... "They can talk about all their old time hockey games, but those boys of mine are the greatest ever."

THE TRADITION

DETROIT
RED WINGS

1942-43
STANLEY
CUP
CHAMPIONS

THE TEAM

COACH: Ebbie Goodfellow (player/coach).

HALL OF FAMERS (6): Sid Abel, Jack Adams (manager), Goodfellow, Syd Howe, Jack Stewart, Harry Watson.

TOP PLAYERS: C Abel (49 games, 18-24 – 42), RW Mud Bruneteau (50 games, 23-22 – 45), RW Joe Carveth (43 games, 18-18 – 36), F Howe (50 games, 20-35 – 55), LW Carl Liscombe (50 games, 19-23 – 42), D Jimmy Orlando (40 games, 3-4 – 7, 99 PIM), D Stewart * (44 games, 2-9 – 11), LW Watson (50 games, 13-18 – 31).

GOALIE: Johnny Mowers * (50 games, 25 wins, 6 shutouts, 2.47 goals-against average, Vezina Trophy).

* Postseason All-Star.

THE SEASON

TEAM	W	L	T	PTS
Detroit	25	14	11	61
Boston	24	17	9	57
Toronto	22	19	9	53
Montreal	19	19	12	50
Chicago	17	18	15	49
New York	11	31	8	30

THE PLAYOFFS

ROUND ONE: Detroit eliminated Toronto, 4-2.

CUP FINALS: Detroit eliminated Boston, 4-0.

THE FINALS

GAME 1: Detroit 6, Boston 2.

GAME 2: Detroit 4, Boston 3.

GAME 3: Detroit 4, Boston 0.

GAME 4: Detroit 2, Boston 0. Winning goal: Joe Carveth.

1942-43

Wings ride Mowers to sweep of Bruins, return Cup to Detroit

April 8, 1943

BY JOHN N. SABO

BOSTON, April 8 — All the glory that goes with the highest of hockey prizes — the Stanley Cup — today belongs to the Detroit Red Wings.

They earned it tonight in as brilliant a finish to a championship drive as has ever been staged. The Wings climbed onto the golden throne by whitewashing the badly outplayed Boston Bruins, 2 to 0, in the fourth and clinching contest before 12,954 sad Bostonians.

This was a great ending to a furious drive for the Stanley Cup which now comes back to Detroit for the first time since 1937 and the third time in Red Wings history.

Standing right at the head of this championship Detroit team is Goalie Johnny Mowers. Tonight Mowers was nothing short of spectacular. He blocked everything the Bruins had to toss at him — and that was plenty — to score his second shutout in as many nights.

... Sharing top honors on this championship night for the Wings were Carl Liscombe and Joe Carveth. They were the boys who produced the two goals, both on solo dashes smacking of a Hollywood movie thriller.

This triumph in four straight over the Bruins, capped by two shutouts in two nights right in Boston Gardens, makes ample amends for the indignity the Wings suffered two years ago when another Bruin team beat them four straight in the playoffs.

DETROIT FREE PRESS FILE PHOTO

Before Gordie, Detroit had another Hall of Fame Howe — Syd Howe. Syd scored 20 goals in the championship season.

1949-50

TONY SPINA

Ted Lindsay, left, and Gordie Howe had plenty to smile about after helping Detroit win its first Cup since 1943.

First-ever Game 7 overtime ends with Wings' fourth Cup

April 23, 1950

BY MARSHALL DANN

The Stanley Cup has come back to Detroit for the first time since 1943.

On a dramatic overtime goal by Pete Babando, a "poor cousin" on the Detroit squad most of the season, the Wings scored a 4-3 victory in the seventh and deciding game of the finals against the New York Rangers.

The path to the Cup was rocky, and the last mile was the roughest. The Wings fought an uphill battle for the second straight night to pull a game out of the fire.

Trailing 2 to 0 in the first period, they erupted for three goals in the second period to tie the count at 3-all. Then the teams played scoreless hockey for more than 52 minutes before Babando came through.

The end came at 12:14 a.m. Monday with Babando slapping home a backhand shot from 15 feet after 28:31 of overtime play.

It was the second goal of the game for Babando, who was shunted to the role of bench warmer for most of the series.

Detroit's other tallies were from Sid Abel and Jimmy McFadden, while Al Stanley, Tony Leswick and Buddy O'Connor paraded goalward in that order for New York.

... It marked the first time in Cup history that a seventh and deciding game went into overtime. But then, these playoffs have been wacky all along.

Detroit went the full seven games in the semifinal against Toronto, winning the sixth and seventh games to survive.

... This was the fourth time Detroit has won the Stanley Cup, but the 13,095 fans at Olympia Sunday were the first ever to witness a presentation on home ice.

THE TEAM

COACH: Tommy Ivan.

HALL OF FAMERS (9): Sid Abel, Jack Adams (manager), Gordie Howe, Ivan, Red Kelly, Ted Lindsay, Harry Lumley, Marcel Pronovost, Jack Stewart.

TOP PLAYERS: C Abel * (69 games 34-35 – 69), RW Howe * (70 games, 35-33 – 68), D Kelly * (70 games, 15-25 – 40), LW Lindsay * (69 games, 23-55 – 78, Art Ross Trophy), D Leo Reise Jr. * (70 games, 4-17 – 21).

GOALIE: Lumley (63 games, 33 wins, 7 shutouts, 2.35 goals-against average).

* Postseason All-Star.

THE SEASON

TEAM	W	L	T	PTS
Detroit	37	19	14	88
Montreal	29	22	19	77
Toronto	31	27	12	74
New York	28	31	11	67
Boston	22	32	16	60
Chicago	22	38	10	54

THE PLAYOFFS

ROUND ONE: Detroit eliminated Toronto, 4-3.

CUP FINALS: Detroit eliminated New York, 4-3.

THE FINALS

GAME 1: Detroit 4, New York 1.

GAME 2: New York 3, Detroit 1.

GAME 3: Detroit 4, New York 0.

GAME 4: New York 4, Detroit 3 (OT).

GAME 5: New York 2, Detroit 1 (OT).

GAME 6: Detroit 5, New York 4.

GAME 7: Detroit 4, New York 3 (2OT). Winning goal: Pete Babando.

THE TRADITION

DETROIT
RED WINGS

1951-52
STANLEY
CUP
CHAMPIONS

1951-52

THE TEAM

COACH: Tommy Ivan.

HALL OF FAMERS (9):
Sid Abel, Jack Adams (manager), Alex Delvecchio, Gordie Howe, Ivan, Red Kelly, Ted Lindsay, Marcel Pronovost, Terry Sawchuk.

TOP PLAYERS: C Abel (62 games, 17-36 – 53), C Delvecchio (65 games, 15-22 – 37), D Bob Goldham (69 games, 0-14 – 14), RW Howe * (70 games, 47-39 – 86, Art Ross Trophy, Hart Trophy) * D Kelly * (67 games, 16-31 – 47), LW Lindsay * (70 games, 30-39 – 69), C Metro Prystai (69 games, 21-22 – 43).

GOALIE: Sawchuk * (70 games, 44 wins, 12 shutouts, 1.90 goals-against average, Vezina Trophy).

* Postseason All-Star.

THE SEASON

TEAM	W	L	T	PTS
Detroit	44	14	12	100
Montreal	34	26	10	78
Toronto	29	25	16	74
Boston	25	29	16	66
New York	23	34	13	59
Chicago	17	44	9	43

THE PLAYOFFS

ROUND ONE: Detroit eliminated Toronto, 4-0.

CUP FINALS: Detroit eliminated Montreal, 4-0.

THE FINALS

GAME 1: Detroit 3, Montreal 1.

GAME 2: Detroit 2, Montreal 1.

GAME 3: Detroit 3, Montreal 0.

GAME 4: Detroit 3, Montreal 0. Winning goal: Metro Prystai.

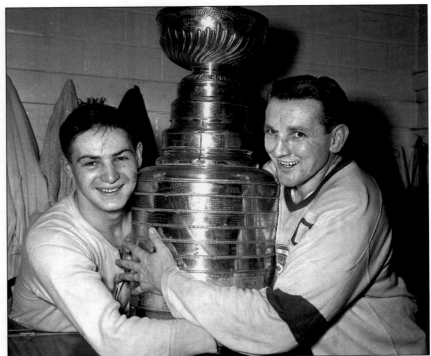

PRESTON STROUP/ASSOCIATED PRESS

Captain Sid Abel, right, and Terry Sawchuk had the Cup in their grasp, thanks mainly to Sawchuk's great goaltending.

Sawchuk leads way as Wings rocket to perfect postseason

April 15, 1952

BY MARSHALL DANN

Swoosh!

That was the Detroit Red Wings sweeping first through the Toronto Maple Leafs then the Montreal Canadiens in eight straight Stanley Cup playoff games to make National Hockey League history.

The clincher over Montreal was applied Tuesday night, 3 to 0, before 14,545 Olympia fans who came expecting just such an ending and cheered every minute of it.

Coming after the 11-game margin by which Detroit posted its fourth straight league title, victory left the 1951-52 Wings stamped beyond question as one of the greatest teams in hockey history.

It was Terry Sawchuk's series, and the brilliant sophomore goalie finished it in style. Tuesday's was his fourth shutout in the eight games, giving him a string of goose-eggs for all four games played on home ice.

... When the siren ended the game, a wild and impromptu celebration broke out on the ice with Sawchuk the center of it all.

He had tied the all-time playoff record with his four shutouts, matching performances previously posted by Toronto's Frank McCool and New York's Dave Kerr.

... It marked the fifth time the cup has come here, the previous settings being 1936, 1937, 1943, and 1950.

... But none of the ceremonies ever was more enthusiastic. Detroit had just earned the three-foot mug which has meant supremacy of all of hockey for the last 58 years with a smoothness never seen in the previous 57.

First came four straight over arch-rival Toronto by 3-0, 1-0, 6-2 and 3-1 scores. Then came four more against the second-place Canadiens by 3-1, 2-1, 3-0 and 3-0 margins.

Some day a team may tie that record, but no one ever can beat it. Nor has any team ever done it before.

1953-54

DETROIT RED WINGS

1953-54 STANLEY CUP CHAMPIONS

It was close and a cigar for Ted Lindsay, left, Gordie Howe and Alex Delvecchio as the Wings won No. 6 with a 2-1 overtime victory.

Wings dispatch Canadiens in seven to win sixth Cup

April 16, 1954

BY MARSHALL DANN

Tony Leswick was carried off the ice at Olympia on Friday night by Detroit hockey fans and his teammates — the greatest tribute ever paid a Red Wing player as a result of one of the greatest Red Wing victories.

Leswick's goal in sudden-death overtime brought the Stanley Cup back to Detroit for the sixth time.

It ended the seventh and decisive game of the finals against Montreal's defending champions in Detroit's favor, 2 to 1.

The Wings were on the ropes and the record hockey crowd of 15,791 knew it when Leswick fired the decisive shot after 4:29 of overtime action.

... That shot suddenly became the biggest goal of the entire 1953-54 season. It slipped cleanly over (Montreal goalie Gerry) McNeil's upraised right arm and high into the Montreal cage.

... Some may claim that Detroit got a fluke victory on a screen shot.

But that was the way Montreal scored its lone goal to take the lead midway in the first period. Floyd Curry directed it from 50 feet out and Terry Sawchuk was screened all the way.

Red Kelly got the equalizer early in the second stanza on a clean power-play drive. Alex Delvecchio and Ted Lindsay handled the relays which set up Kelly 15 feet off the left side of the cage.

Those were the scoring plays of the game which crowned Detroit the dual champion of hockey. Linked with the Stanley Cup triumph was the Wings' sixth straight National League championship.

But the scoring plays didn't cover all the stars of the game. Terry Sawchuk stands foremost among the others — not only for his play in the finale but also in the 11 previous playoff contests.

THE TEAM

COACH: Tommy Ivan. Hall of Famers (9): Jack Adams (manager), Al Arbour, Alex Delvecchio, Gordie Howe, Ivan, Red Kelly, Ted Lindsay, Marcel Pronovost, Terry Sawchuk.

TOP PLAYERS: C Delvecchio (69 games, 11-18 – 29), RW Howe * (70 games, 33-48 –81, Art Ross Trophy), D Kelly * (62 games, 16-33 – 49, Norris Trophy, Lady Byng), LW Lindsay * (70 games, 26-36-62), D Pronovost (57 games, 6-12 – 18).

GOALIE: Sawchuk * (67 games, 35 wins, 12 shutouts, 1.93 goals-against average).

* Postseason All-Star.

THE SEASON

TEAM	W	L	T	PTS
Detroit	37	19	14	88
Montreal	35	24	11	81
Toronto	32	24	14	78
Boston	32	28	10	74
New York	29	31	10	68
Chicago	12	51	7	31

THE PLAYOFFS

ROUND ONE: Detroit eliminated Toronto, 4-1.

CUP FINALS: Detroit eliminated Montreal, 4-3.

THE FINALS

GAME 1: Detroit 3, Montreal 1.

GAME 2: Montreal 3, Detroit 1.

GAME 3: Detroit 5, Montreal 2.

GAME 4: Detroit 2, Montreal 0.

GAME 5: Montreal 1, Detroit 0 (OT).

GAME 6: Montreal 4, Detroit 1.

GAME 7: Detroit 2, Montreal 1 (OT). Winning goal: Tony Leswick.

THE TEAM

COACH: Jimmy Skinner.

HALL OF FAMERS (7): Jack Adams (manager), Alex Delvecchio, Gordie Howe, Red Kelly, Ted Lindsay, Marcel Pronovost, Terry Sawchuk.

TOP PLAYERS: LW Delvecchio (69 games, 17-31 – 48), D Bob Goldham * (69 games, 1-16 – 17), RW Howe (64 games, 29-33 – 62), D Kelly * (70 games, 15-30 – 45), LW Lindsay (49 games, 19-19 – 38), C Earl Reibel (70 games, 25-41 – 66).

GOALIE: Sawchuk * (68 games, 40 wins, 12 shutouts, 1.94 goals-against average, Vezina Trophy).

* Postseason All-Star.

THE SEASON

TEAM	W	L	T	PTS
Detroit	42	17	11	95
Montreal	41	18	11	93
Toronto	24	24	22	70
Boston	23	26	21	67
New York	17	35	18	52
Chicago	13	40	17	43

THE PLAYOFFS

ROUND ONE: Detroit eliminated Toronto, 4-0.

CUP FINALS: Detroit eliminated Montreal, 4-3.

THE FINALS

GAME 1: Detroit 4, Montreal 2.

GAME 2: Detroit 7, Montreal 1.

GAME 3: Montreal 4, Detroit 2.

GAME 4: Montreal 5, Detroit 3.

GAME 5: Detroit 5, Montreal 1.

GAME 6: Montreal 6, Detroit 3.

GAME 7: Detroit 3, Montreal 1. Winning goal: Gordie Howe.

ASSOCIATED PRESS

Goalie Terry Sawchuk was just one of the Hall of Famers on the roster as the Wings won their seventh Stanley Cup.

Howe's winner sends Wings to victory in shootout series

April 14, 1955

BY MARSHALL DANN

The Red Wings got the Stanley Cup — and handshakes, too, this time.

The handshaking scene between the victorious Red Wings and the conquered Montreal Canadiens was witnessed by 15,541 Olympia fans Thursday night.

… Alex Delvecchio, in the "doghouse" midway in the season, blazed in two goals.

Perennial star Gordie Howe sandwiched another one in, and it became the winner when Floyd Curry finally ruined Terry Sawchuk's shutout late in the game.

Thus, with one more momentous clutch victory, Detroit claimed its seventh Stanley Cup in history.

No one has won more. Toronto and Montreal also have taken seven.

… Everything was as it was a year ago when Detroit took the cup in another seven-game finals against the Canadiens. The same, that is, except for the handshakes.

That year the Canadiens stunned all of Canada by failing to make the customary sportsmanlike maneuver.

This time Tom Johnson, a fierce competitor, led the rush to congratulate the Wings. Captain Butch Bouchard was close behind.

The Detroiters heartily returned those handshakes. They knew they'd been through a tough one. The Canadiens never yielded and never quit.

The series was one for the record books with its 47 goals — the most in cup history. Twice the inspired Canadiens came from behind to tie the score; once after Detroit took a 2-0 lead and again when Detroit had a 3-2 victory edge.

That forced the big No. 7, and Detroit once more proved itself the greatest "big game" team hockey has seen.

By winning the clutch games, Detroit has won seven straight National League titles and four Stanley Cups over the same span.

1996-97

DETROIT
RED WINGS

1996-97
STANLEY
CUP
CHAMPIONS

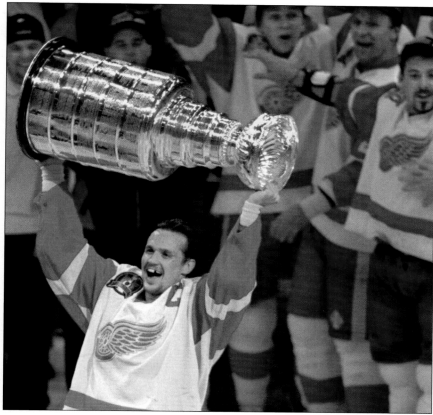

The Captain hoisted the Cup during the victory party that was 42 years in the making and then got to take it home after the game.

JULIAN H. GONZALEZ

THE TEAM

COACH: Scotty Bowman.

HALL OF FAMERS (2): Bowman, Slava Fetisov.

TOP PLAYERS:
C Sergei Fedorov (74 games, 30-33 – 63),
D Vladimir Konstantinov (77 games, 5-33 – 38),
D Nicklas Lidstrom (79 games, 15-42 – 57),
LW Brendan Shanahan (81 games, 47-41 – 88),
C Steve Yzerman (81 games, 22-63 – 85).

GOALIES: Chris Osgood (47 games, 23 wins, 6 shutouts, 2.30 goals-against average), Mike Vernon (33 games, 13 wins, 2.43 goals-against average, Conn Smythe Trophy).

THE SEASON
(Top six teams)

TEAM	W	L	T	PTS
Colo.	49	24	9	107
Dallas	48	26	8	104
N.J.	45	23	14	104
Phila.	45	24	13	103
Detroit	38	26	18	94
Buffalo	40	30	12	92

THE PLAYOFFS

ROUND ONE: Detroit eliminated St. Louis, 4-2.

ROUND TWO: Detroit eliminated Anaheim, 4-0.

ROUND THREE: Detroit eliminated Colorado, 4-2.

CUP FINALS: Detroit eliminated Philadelphia, 4-0.

THE FINALS

GAME 1: Detroit 4, Philadelphia 2.

GAME 2: Detroit 4, Philadelphia 2.

GAME 3: Detroit 6, Philadelphia 1.

GAME 4: Detroit 2, Philadelphia 1. Winning goal: Darren McCarty.

After 42 years of futility, Wings bring Cup back to Detroit

June 7, 1997

BY JASON LA CANFORA

The future Hall of Famer emerged from Joe Louis Arena about 3:15 Sunday morning, carrying the one thing he had waited all his life to earn.

Steve Yzerman, the Red Wings' captain for 11 years, strutted out of the dressing room with the Stanley Cup held above his head, walked into the players' parking lot, placed the Cup in the backseat, jumped in his Porsche, and drove off as a handful of fans roared outside.

Two generations have passed since a Red Wing hoisted the Cup, kissed it, paraded it around the ice and handed it to his teammates and coaches. Yzerman's departure brought to a close one of the wildest nights in Detroit history, one of the biggest parties in 42 years — the last time the Wings won the Cup.

"I don't know how to describe it," he said. "I'm glad the game is over, but I wish it never ended."

... There was so much to savor. The memories will last a lifetime. The score of Game 4 of the Stanley Cup finals, 2-1, might be forgotten. The goal-scorers, Nicklas Lidstrom and Darren McCarty — he of the Cup-clincher — could get lost in the telling of this tale to future generations.

... The frustration was finally lifted at 10:50 on Saturday night. The Philadelphia Flyers were defeated, the horn blew, the pounds of confetti fell to the ice, the fireworks went off — startling coach Scotty Bowman, already wearing his Stanley Cup champions cap.

Helmets, gloves, sticks and pads were sent skyward and scattered all over the ice. The bench emptied and a mass of Red Wings engulfed goalie Mike Vernon, the Conn Smythe winner as playoffs MVP.

DETROIT RED WINGS

1997-98 STANLEY CUP CHAMPIONS

THE TEAM

COACH: Scotty Bowman.

HALL OF FAMERS (2): Bowman, Slava Fetisov.

TOP PLAYERS:
C Sergei Fedorov (21 games, 6-11 – 17),
LW Slava Kozlov (80 games, 25-27 – 52),
C Igor Larionov (69 games, 8-39 – 47),
D Nicklas Lidstrom * (80 games, 17-42 – 59),
D Larry Murphy (82 games, 11-41 – 52),
LW Brendan Shanahan (75 games, 28-29 – 57),
C Steve Yzerman (75 games, 24-45 – 69, Conn Smythe Trophy).

GOALIE: Chris Osgood (64 games, 33 wins, 6 shutouts, 2.21 goals-against average).

* Postseason All-Star.

THE SEASON
(Top seven teams)

TEAM	W	L	T	PTS
Dallas	49	22	11	109
N.J.	48	23	11	107
Detroit	44	23	15	103
St. Louis	45	29	8	98
Pitt.	40	24	18	98
Phila.	42	29	11	95
Colo.	39	26	17	95

THE PLAYOFFS

ROUND ONE: Detroit eliminated Phoenix, 4-2.

ROUND TWO: Detroit eliminated St. Louis, 4-2.

ROUND THREE: Detroit eliminated Dallas, 4-2.

CUP FINALS: Detroit eliminated Washington, 4-0.

THE FINALS

GAME 1: Detroit 2, Washington 1.

GAME 2: Detroit 5, Washington 4 (OT).

GAME 3: Detroit 2, Washington 1.

GAME 4: Detroit 4, Washington 1. Winning goal: Martin Lapointe.

1997-98

Wings sweep Capitals to reclaim Cup for Vladdie

June 16, 1998

BY JASON LA CANFORA

WASHINGTON — He was wheeled through the concourse with 8½ minutes left in the season, no longer able to play, no longer able to walk on his own.

His Red Wings teammates had a second consecutive Stanley Cup well in hand. A sweep of the Washington Capitals was certain.

It was time for Vladimir Konstantinov to celebrate.

He was wheeled onto the ice, and trainer John Wharton rushed to greet him. The Wings were shaking hands with the Capitals, the series wrapped up with a 4-1 victory.

"Vlad-die! Vlad-die! Vlad-die!"

The MCI Center roared its salute, and the Wings gathered around their fallen teammate, the fearless leader who was a demon on the ice for them one year ago, before he nearly died in a limousine accident in June 1997.

Konstantinov pulled a cigar to his mouth and raised his index finger. He and his buddies were indeed No. 1 again.

Captain Steve Yzerman, the Conn Smythe Trophy winner as playoff MVP, raised the Cup first, as he did last year, then put it on Konstantinov's lap. Everyone gathered for a group photo, Vladdie sporting his 1998 Stanley Cup champions cap.

"This is Vladdie's Cup," Igor Larionov said. "I know he could enjoy it. He understood what was going on. He'll come back and walk again on his own. He'll lead a normal life. I know it."

Wharton said: "This Cup wasn't for Vladdie and Sergei, it was because of them."

The ninth Stanley Cup in the Wings' 72-year history belongs to Konstantinov and Sergei Mnatsakanov as much as anyone. The former All-Star defenseman and the massage therapist were robbed of their livelihoods, and nearly their lives, on June 13, 1997.

But no one can take June 16, 1998, away.

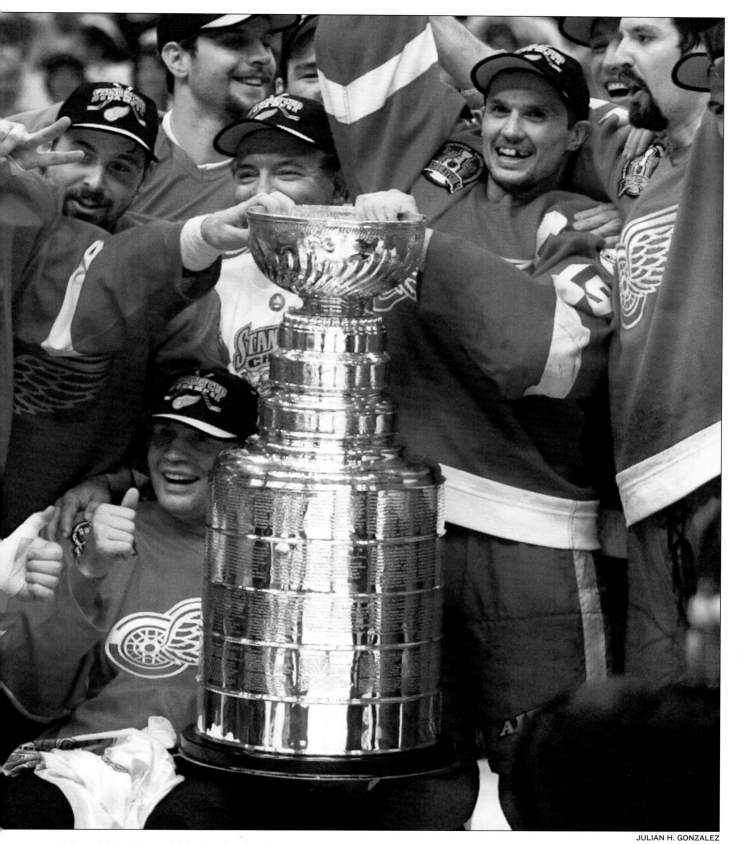

Although Vladdie couldn't play for the Cup, his teammates let him know he was part of their second straight championship.

J. KYLE KEENER

Building a Champion

Great expectations

BY NICHOLAS J. COTSONIKA

It was April 2001, and the Winged Wheels had fallen off the bandwagon. The Red Wings had lost to Los Angeles in the first round of the playoffs, and some were discouraged so much by the downward trend — Stanley Cups in 1997 and 1998, second-round losses in 1999 and 2000 — they said it was time to break up the team.

"I remember thinking to myself, 'The team's not ready for that,'" Brendan Shanahan said. "Why would anyone in this city want that? This is a great time to be a hockey player and a hockey fan in the city of Detroit. You want that to last as long as possible. Talk to people in Edmonton, on Long Island. They miss those days, when it was a hot, hot ticket."

Now the only people who want to break up this team live in other NHL cities.

The Wings didn't get any younger in the off-season. In fact, they got older. Fourteen players were at least 30. One was 40. But they also got better.

They added Dominik Hasek, who won his sixth Vezina Trophy as the NHL's best goaltender in 2001. They added Luc Robitaille, who scored five more goals in 2000-01 than any Wing did. Then they added Brett Hull, who scored two more goals in 2000-01 than Robitaille did. Along the way, they made another addition, defenseman Fredrik Olausson, and several subtractions.

Just look at the lineup and its nine potential Hall of Famers: Hasek, Hull, Robitaille, Shanahan, Chris Chelios, Sergei Fedorov, Igor Larionov, Nicklas Lidstrom and Steve Yzerman.

And the coach, Scotty Bowman, who has won more games than anyone else, already was in the Hall of Fame. Had been for a decade.

"We're talking household names," general manager Ken Holland said, "and a number of them."

"These," Darren McCarty said, "are icons of the sport."

There never was a team like this one. Entering the season, these players had made 25 first or second postseason All-Star teams, won 27 major individual postseason awards, combined for 60 All-Star Game appearances and combined for 90 hat tricks. Four of the top 10 active goal-scorers and three of the top 10 active overall scorers were on this team.

It wasn't always this way. Joe

Voice of the fans

It was early October, three days before the Wings' home opener. Some players heard it themselves that Monday night. The rest heard about it the next day in the dressing room.

As the Lions stumbled to a 35-0 loss to St. Louis and an 0-3 record, desperate fans at the Silverdome started chanting, "Let's go, Red Wings!" And then "Monday Night Football" funnyman Dennis Miller cracked that the fans wanted Wings great Alex Delvecchio at quarterback.

"I was sitting there, lying in bed, and I started hearing it," Kris Draper said. "It was as clear as day, too. I knew exactly what was going on." Added Darren McCarty, "That's as close as I'm going to get to getting on 'Monday Night Football.'"

But the Wings understood what the chant meant. The Tigers had suffered through another losing season, the Lions were hopeless and the Pistons' prospects were uncertain. "Everybody's frustrated in a lot of ways," McCarty said. "Hopefully, we can bring them some enjoyment."

Dominik Hasek was the centerpiece of the rebuilding process after the Red Wings were stunned by the Los Angeles Kings in the first round of the 2001 playoffs.

Louis Arena had been sold out since the mid-1980s. There were about 17,000 season-ticket holders. There was a waiting list. But when Mike Ilitch bought the team and hired Jimmy Devellano as general manager in 1982, the average crowd size was about 7,000. There were 2,100 season-ticket holders. Not only was there no waiting list, there was no waiting for anything. Concessions? Bathroom? Step right up. By the end of the 1982-83 season, the Wings had missed the playoffs for five straight years and 12 times in 13 years.

"It was not Hockeytown," said Devellano, senior vice president. "The fans had left the team. It was pretty apparent that we really now had to do something to sell tickets, had to somehow give the fans and the press something with a little more hope, something with a little more pizzazz."

In 1983, the Red Wings drafted Yzerman and signed Brad Park, a six-time runner-up for the Norris Trophy as the league's best defenseman. The next year, they traded for Darryl Sittler, a fan favorite in Toronto, the Leafs' all-time leading scorer. Other stars came and went.

There was Borje Salming, the first European star in the NHL, a two-time Norris runner-up; Bernie Federko, a renowned playmaker; Jimmy Carson, a Detroit native who had scored 55 goals one season; Dino Ciccarelli, a scrappy character, the ninth man to score 600 goals; Mark Howe, son of Gordie, a three-time Norris runner-up.

When the Wings improved to the point where they were competing annually for the Cup, they brought in more names. There was Paul Coffey, the second-highest scoring defenseman of all-time, who won one of his three Norris trophies with the Wings; Mike Vernon, who won the 1997 Conn Smythe Trophy as playoff MVP; Slava Fetisov, the legendary Red Army captain; Larry

KIRTHMON F. DOZIER

Sniper Brett Hull (17) was signed to give the Red Wings enough firepower to get them past the likes of Patrick Roy and the 2001 champion Colorado Avalanche.

Murphy, second in games played to Gordie Howe, the third-highest scoring defenseman all-time. Larionov. Shanahan. The Wings brought them in to put them over the top.

"We've felt that maybe with the right move or two we'd have the chance to do it," Devellano said. "We've just been so damn good. How the heck do you not keep trying to add one or two more pieces?"

Championship teams are supposed to decline. That's the way leagues are structured. The bad teams draft first, the good teams last. The bad teams are supposed to get better, the good teams worse. The standings are due to flip. But the Wings have stayed on top.

Entering the 2001-02 season, they had won more games in the regular season (363) and playoffs (70) than any other team over the past eight years. No one had won more Cups since 1990. Only three of 30 teams — Colorado, New Jersey and Pittsburgh — had won as many.

The Wings brought in Chris

Chelios, a three-time Norris winner, and Pat Verbeek, the only player to have 500 goals and 2,500 penalty minutes. They brought in Hasek, Hull and Robitaille.

"In a lot of towns, people accuse the owners and management of not trying to win," Devellano said. "That's the one thing no one's been able to accuse us of. That's the one thing we've constantly tried to do. So far, so good."

In March 2001, Ilitch said he would do "whatever's necessary" to keep the Wings in contention for the Cup. "Once the city gets used to it, you get used to it," Ilitch said. "You've got to pay the price. ... We've got to do anything we can. The Red Wings are so much a part of the city now, you just want to keep it that way."

And he kept his word. The Wings' payroll was one of the highest in the league — about $65 million. Detroit might be a small market in other sports, but in hockey it's a big-market bully. The Wings can land big-ticket free agents and acquire players other teams no longer can afford.

What is remarkable is the sacrifices fans, ownership and players have made to make it happen. The fans shell out $51 to $80 for most seats at the Joe. And that's just during the regular season. In the playoffs, we're talking multiples of that. But basically, the Wings pass the money right along to the players. Almost all of what they bring in, they turn around and spend.

The Wings let it be known they would not turn a profit unless they advanced deep into the playoffs. "We need a heck of a run," Devellano said before the season. "It can't be a first-round ouster, that's for sure, or we struck out and it's going to be quite a hit. We're taking a risk most people couldn't or wouldn't do."

"There are a lot of owners and organizations that would take money and profit and put it right in their pocket," Shanahan said.

"Here, it seems to always be reinvested, put toward continuing the love affair between the team and the city."

But money can't buy championships. Otherwise, the New York Rangers would have the Cup every year. To bring together a line-up of stars like this, the stars have to align.

When the Wings won four Cups in six years in the 1950s, their boss, Jack Adams, scoffed at writers who compared the Wings to the New York Yankees: "We are not the Yankees of hockey — the Yankees are the Red Wings of baseball," he said. Devellano won't go that far, but he doesn't downplay the comparison.

"We're very similar to the New York Yankees, even to the point where a lot of people get ticked off at us," Devellano said. "A lot of people get jealous, just as they're all jealous of the Yankees."

One more thing: Both the Wings and the Yankees faced incredible expectations. In 2000-01, the Wings finished with 111 points, second-most in the league and in franchise history. But because they lost in the first round of the playoffs, the season was a deep disappointment.

"We understand that's the nature of the beast," Devellano said. "This is a franchise people are very passionate about now. We've created that. That's a good thing. . . . Those are expectations we just have to try to live up to."

"When a team goes out and supplies you with this type of group to work with, it's up to the group to go out and do the job," Shanahan said. "It's not just enough to have a certain amount of career goals or to have played in a certain amount of All-Star Games. We have to translate it into wins. Otherwise, the names mean nothing."

In the end, after all the superlatives, all the hype, all the money, the Red Wings drank from the Cup. If they hadn't, an entire town would've been left thirsty.

KIRTHMON F. DOZIER

MITCH ALBOM

Mr. Holland's opus

A general manager is neither player nor coach. He doesn't skate or knock away pucks. He doesn't blow a whistle. What he does, in a front-office sort of way, is paint. He paints a portrait of a team he wants. He paints faces over each roster spot and finally, when all the trading and cutting and buying are over, he leans back to examine his canvas.

The Red Wings have perhaps the most impressive canvas in NHL history. And Ken Holland, the GM, the man who more than anyone painted their faces over the roster spots, watched ner-vously to see how his master-piece came together.

Mr. Holland's Opus.

"Is it the best team you've ever helped assemble?" Holland was asked before the playoffs. "You can't say yet," he answered. "It's the most high-profile. Maybe the most talent. But the best team is always the one that wins the Stanley Cup."

Consider the roster: Steve Yzerman, Brett Hull and Luc Robitaille — all with more than 600 career goals, three of the top 10 scorers of all time. Brendan Shanahan, Sergei Fedorov and

Igor Larionov, all Salt Lake Olympians and multi-time All-Stars, all in the front lines. Nicklas Lidstrom and Chris Chelios on defense, the Norris Trophy winner and one of the best plus-minus forces in the league. And, backing them up, Dominik Hasek, considered by many goalie-watchers to be tops in the business. And that's without mentioning Kris Draper or Pavel Datsyuk or Darren McCarty, Kirk Maltby, Tomas Holmstrom, Boyd Devereaux, Jiri Fischer. . . .

Mr. Holland's Opus.

As paintings go, it's Realist and Impressionist. As in real impressive.

But why did it work? Holland has a theory: "Obviously, when we got Dominik, we knew we were going to have to move Chris Osgood. So we knew Dom would have that position outright. But in bringing in Brett Hull and Luc Robitaille, you never know. These were guys who had been really high-profile on their team, and with all the guys we have here, they weren't going to have the same roles they had before, maybe not be on as many power plays, not get as many goals or as much ice time.

"But in talking to both of those players, and their agents, it was so clear they wanted to come here. In fact, Hull did things with his contract to make it possible. And other guys on our team" — Yzerman, Lidstrom, Shanahan and Chelios — "did things with their contracts to make it possible as well. That's when I knew we had a really good chance at the chemistry you need to be successful."

The financial trade-offs are part of what made the locker room as relaxed and familiar as a high school reunion, a rock band's jam session or a Friday night poker game in your buddy's basement.

There were quieter guys (Yzerman, Lidstrom) and louder guys (Hull, McCarty) and foreign guys (Hasek, Fedorov, Holmstrom, etc.), and it just seemed to all come together.

"After we lost (to Los Angeles) last year," Holland said, "I talked to Mr. Ilitch. He said he was willing to spend if the moves would make us better. Right now, I'd say there's a lot of teams out there that are envious of the commitment of our ownership."

Not to mention the team picture. It's Mr. Holland's Opus. A portrait of talent. A canvas of dreams. It cost a lot, but it paid off.

How the Wings were built

NO.	POS	NAME	HOW ACQUIRED
42	LW	Sean Avery	Signed as free agent, Sept. 21, 1999.
24	D	Chris Chelios	Acquired from Chicago for Anders Eriksson and 1999 and 2001 first-round draft choices, March 23, 1999.
11	D	Mathieu Dandenault	Drafted by Red Wings in 1994 (second choice, 49th overall).
13	C	Pavel Datsyuk	Drafted by Red Wings in 1998 (eighth choice, 171st overall).
21	C	Boyd Devereaux	Signed as unrestricted free agent, Aug. 23, 2000.
33	C	Kris Draper	Acquired from Winnipeg for future considerations, June 30, 1993.
28	D	Steve Duchesne	Signed as free agent, Sept. 4, 1999.
38	G	Jason Elliott	Drafted by Red Wings in 1994 (seventh choice, 205th overall).
91	C	Sergei Fedorov	Drafted by Red Wings in 1989 (fourth choice, 74th overall).
2	D	Jiri Fischer	Drafted by Red Wings in 1998 (first choice, 25th overall).
39	G	Dominik Hasek	Acquired from Buffalo for Slava Kozlov and 2002 first-round draft choice, July 1, 2001.
96	LW	Tomas Holmstrom	Drafted by Red Wings in 1994 (ninth choice, 257th overall).
17	RW	Brett Hull	Signed as free agent, Aug. 22, 2001.
15	LW	Ladislav Kohn	Signed as free agent, Oct. 5, 2001.
4	D	Uwe Krupp	Signed as free agent, July 7, 1998.
32	D	Maxim Kuznetsov	Drafted by Red Wings in 1995 (first choice, 26th overall).
8	C	Igor Larionov	Acquired from Florida for Yan Golubovsky, Dec. 28, 2000.
34	G	Manny Legace	Signed as free agent, July 16, 1999.
5	D	Nicklas Lidstrom	Drafted by Red Wings in 1989 (third choice, 53rd overall).
18	RW	Kirk Maltby	Acquired from Edmonton for Dan McGillis, March 20, 1996.
25	RW	Darren McCarty	Drafted by Red Wings in 1992 (second choice, 46th overall).
27	D	Fredrik Olausson	Signed as free agent, May 30, 2001.
20	LW	Luc Robitaille	Signed as free agent, July 2, 2001.
14	LW	Brendan Shanahan	Acquired from Hartford with Brian Glynn for Keith Primeau, Paul Coffey and 1997 first-round draft choice, Oct. 9, 1996.
71	D	Jiri Slegr	Acquired from Atlanta for Yuri Butsayev and 2002 third-round draft choice, March 19, 2002.
3	D	Jesse Wallin	Drafted by Red Wings in 1996 (first choice, 26th overall).
29	C	Jason Williams	Signed as free agent, Sept. 18, 2000.
19	C	Steve Yzerman	Drafted by Red Wings in 1983 (first choice, fourth overall).

KIRTHMON F. DOZIER

Rookie Pavel Datsyuk was drafted by the Red Wings in 1998 and saw significant ice time this season.

MANDI WRIGHT

A Season of Milestones

One to remember

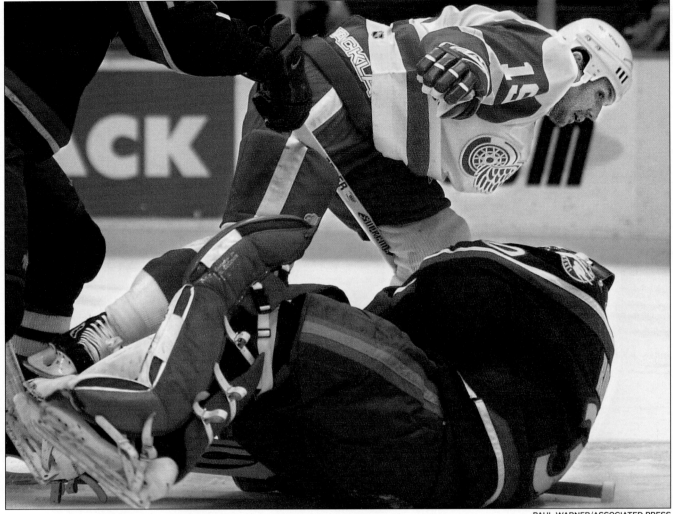

PAUL WARNER/ASSOCIATED PRESS

Steve Yzerman victimized Minnesota's Dwayne Roloson for his milestone 650th and 651st goals.

BY HELENE ST. JAMES

Steve Yzerman looked up at the scoreboard, shook his head and laughed. A fan had just picked the wrong answer to the question of who assisted on Yzerman's first NHL goal.

Half an hour later, Yzerman gave the fan an easier bit of trivia to remember: Who set up his 650th?

It was Brendan Shanahan who, early in the second period, slipped the puck to Yzerman just inside the Minnesota blue line. Yzerman grabbed it and fired a shot into the top corner, reaching another milestone in a rich career.

Nine minutes later, he scored again as the Red Wings posted an 8-3 rout of the Wild at Joe Louis Arena. For good measure, Yzerman set up Luc Robitaille's 601st goal later in the second period.

Robitaille finished with two goals, Brett Hull reached 1,200 career points off two assists, and Fredrik Olausson and Pavel Datsyuk also had two helpers each.

Tomas Holmstrom, Nicklas Lidstrom, Shanahan and Boyd Devereaux also scored in the Wings' best offensive output of the season.

"I was encouraged that when it was 5-3 we didn't fall apart," Yzerman said after addressing his milestone with a shrug and a hint of a smile. "But still, there have been too many games where we're allowing goals in the third period."

And just in case the first question comes up again, the answer is Bob Manno and Ed Johnstone, in an Oct. 15, 1983, game at Winnipeg.

A thousand thanks

JULIAN H. GONZALEZ

Mathieu Dandenault (11) made captain Steve Yzerman's 1,000th assist count, cashing it in for the overtime winner against Ottawa.

NHL LEADERS

GOALS

Wayne Gretzky	894
Gordie Howe	801
Marcel Dionne	731
Phil Esposito	717
Mike Gartner	708
Brett Hull *	**679**
Steve Yzerman *	**658**
Mark Messier *	658
Mario Lemieux *	654
Luc Robitaille *	**620**
Bobby Hull	610
Dino Ciccarelli	608
Jari Kurri	601
D. Andreychuk *	593
Mike Bossy	573
Guy Lafleur	560
Johnny Bucyk	556
Michel Goulet	548
Maurice Richard	544
Stan Mikita	541
Frank Mahovlich	533
Bryan Trottier	524
Pat Verbeek *	522
Dale Hawerchuk	518
Gilbert Perreault	512
Jean Beliveau	507
B. Shanahan *	503
Joe Mullen	502
Lanny McDonald	500

ASSISTS

Wayne Gretzky	1,963
Ron Francis *	1,187
Ray Bourque	1,169
Mark Messier *	1,146
Paul Coffey	1,135
Gordie Howe	1,049
Marcel Dionne	1,040
Adam Oates *	1,027
Steve Yzerman *	**1,004**

* active player

OTHER ACTIVE RED WINGS WITH 500 ASSISTS

Chris Chelios	700
Luc Robitaille	668
Brett Hull	567
B. Shanahan	527
Steve Duchesne	525
Sergei Fedorov	507

BY HELENE ST. JAMES

Steve Yzerman became the ninth NHL player with 1,000 assists when he set up Mathieu Dandenault's overtime goal that gave the Red Wings a 3-2 victory over the Ottawa Senators at Joe Louis Arena.

Yzerman chipped the puck into the corner, where it slid behind the net for Igor Larionov, who passed to Dandenault. When Yzerman's name was announced a minute later — after the play had been reviewed because the net was off its moorings — fans jumped to their feet and showered the Captain with "Stevie! Stevie!" as he disappeared down the tunnel and into the locker room.

"I have a lot of respect for the guys who have reached that," Yzerman said of the milestone. "But I look at it that I've played a long time on a good team with a lot of good players, and it's slowly added up. So I don't really look at it as any great achievement."

The assist highlighted a slow game that included 11 minor penalties and a third period in which the Wings outshot the Senators, 21-5. "We're lucky to get a victory out of it because we outshot them, but the quality chances were in their favor," Yzerman said. "I don't think we necessarily feel really good about the game, because we didn't play all that well."

Rookie Pavel Datsyuk got his eighth goal and Luc Robitaille tied it at 2:03 of the third period, finishing a four-shot barrage with his 612th goal two nights after becoming the all-time leading goal-scorer among left wings.

But this night was Yzerman's turn at a milestone. Another puck was collected for history, but if Yzerman should change his mind about keeping it, a teammate stood ready to pounce.

"If he doesn't want it, I'll keep it," Dandenault said. "It's certainly nice to score for Stevie's assist."

'We've got to win'

BY HELENE ST. JAMES

Tucked away somewhere in Steve Yzerman's house is a box that could be worth thousands of dollars on eBay. It contains pucks gathered from the various milestones the Captain has amassed over 19 NHL seasons.

The puck from his 500th goal, scored in January 1996. The ones from his 600th goal, scored in November 1999, and his 650th, scored in November 2001. And the puck that made him the ninth NHL player to record 1,000 assists, a milestone he reached in January 2002.

But for all the personal history he has forged en route to 658 goals and 1,004 assists, two events in Yzerman's career cast the longest shadow.

"We won the Stanley Cup, and those two blow everything else away," he said. "For the first 12-13 years of my career, I was getting all these points and it wasn't good enough, and I recognized that. We've got to win, we've got to win — everybody thought the same thing. We were able to do that. It's the same thing now. Winning is more exciting than the milestones."

And sometimes the milestones come with a snag. When Yzerman notched his 1,000th point, the goal was scored in overtime. By the time his accomplishment was announced over the Joe Louis loudspeakers to the thunderous appreciation of the fans, he wasn't there to hear the cheers.

"Nobody told me what was going on," Yzerman said. "You sit in the locker room and you can't hear anything going on out there. Somebody from the organization should have come down and told me. Eventually Joey Kocur did, but by that time I was standing in a T-shirt and shorts."

Oh, well. He can make up for it when he scores goal No. 700.

JULIAN H. GONZALEZ

Red Wings captain Steve Yzerman has a box full of pucks from various milestones. But another Stanley Cup was worth more than all that rubber.

As for that box — it was misplaced in the aftermath of a house move — Yzerman said he has no plans for its contents. "Every now and then I think a little bit about what I'm going to do with them all."

Precious metals

There was no Rolex watch waiting for Red Wings forward Darren McCarty the day after he scored his 100th goal, in a tie with Chicago on April 10. Instead, the team's public relations staff rewarded him with a stick wrapped in tinfoil.

KIRTHMON F. DOZIER

BY GEORGE SIPPLE

Steve Yzerman brought home the gold, but Darren McCarty was just as proud when he was awarded tin.

Yzerman has had better performances in his long career, but few were more welcome to fans than his emergence from a two-month absence April 10. His return from a right knee injury came on a night when McCarty scored the 100th goal of his career with 5:03 left, capping a two-goal comeback. Sergei Fedorov scored his 30th of the season, and Igor Larionov scored with 6:29 left, forging a 3-3 tie with Chicago.

It was Yzerman's first game since he returned from the Salt Lake Winter Olympics, where he played six games and helped Canada win a gold medal.

McCarty's reward came the next day.

In recent years, the Ilitches have given Red Wings players crystal, Rolex watches and silver sticks to mark their milestone achievements. But when McCarty arrived at his locker before practice, he found a special present: a hockey stick wrapped in tinfoil, courtesy of the public relations staff.

McCarty said he was taking the stick home to hang on his wall.

"Silver for 500 goals . . . 100 is tinfoil," said McCarty, whose toughness usually helps the Wings more than his scoring. "Some of us do other things better."

McCarty said his son, Griffin, was asleep when he scored No. 100. But when McCarty got home, he put the puck next to Griffin's bed.

"Anyone with kids knows when they're excited, you're excited," McCarty said.

600 and counting

PAUL GONZALEZ VIDELA

Luc Robitaille's wife, Stacia, and son Jesse cheer a Red Wings goal against Colorado in the Western Conference finals. The Robitaille family also had reason to cheer when Luc scored his 600th career goal earlier in the season.

BY NICHOLAS J. COTSONIKA

ANAHEIM, Calif. — In vintage style, Luc Robitaille became the 13th NHL player to score 600 goals, as the Red Wings beat the Mighty Ducks, 1-0.

No score. First period. Detroit power play. As Brendan Shanahan wristed the puck from the left point toward the Anaheim net, Robitaille slipped into the low slot. Robitaille tipped the puck out of midair, about waist-high, down and past the right pad of goaltender Jean-Sebastien Giguere. Time: 8:53. History.

The Wings became the first team to have three 600-goal scorers at once — and the three often played on the same line. Steve Yzerman finished the season with 658, Brett Hull 679 and Robitaille 620.

"I saw Shanny had the puck at the blue line," Robitaille said. "When he took that wrister, I just made sure I got in good position to tip it in. I've gotten many in my career like that."

He laughed.

"I guess it's all positioning," he said.

Robitaille received a standing ovation and a hearty "LUUUC!" from the crowd. There were thousands of Wings fans at Arrowhead Pond, as usual. But the rest were just as loud, having appreciated him about 45 minutes or so up the freeway in Los Angeles for 12 of his previous 15 seasons.

"I feel pretty good," Robitaille said. "I mean, I'm happy it's over with, you know? I just wanted to get it as quick as possible and get moving."

Robitaille had places to go. He needed 10 goals to reach the record for left wings, held by Hull's father, Bobby. Robitaille said that mark will mean the most to him. In 1984, he was drafted in the ninth round.

"When you think of that and then you think of being the No. 1 left wing all-time," Robitaille said, "that's going to be pretty special."

A SEASON OF MILESTONES

Give that man a cigar

KIRTHMON F. DOZIER

Brett Hull was the first to congratulate Robitaille on his historic deflection. "A typical goal by me," Robitaille said of No. 611. "I just tipped it into the net."

BY NICHOLAS J. COTSONIKA

ASSOCIATED PRESS FILE PHOTO

Bobby Hull, father of Red Wings forward Brett, was in the stands when Detroit's Luc Robitaille broke the elder Hull's record for goals by a left wing.

History came quickly. One minute, 50 seconds into the Red Wings' 3-1 victory over Washington, Luc Robitaille broke Bobby Hull's record for goals by an NHL left wing.

Kirk Maltby shot from the left point. Just off the left pad of goaltender Olaf Kolzig, just in front of defenseman Brendan Witt, his skates in the crease, Robitaille stuck out his stick. He deflected the puck. And scored No. 611.

"A typical goal by me," Robitaille said. "I just tipped it into the net."

A few minutes later, public address announcer Budd Lynch acknowledged the feat, another milestone moment for what Capitals coach Ron Wilson called a "Hall of Fame team." Players on both sides tapped their sticks against the boards and ice. The fans gave a standing ovation, underscoring it with what has become a common cry of Joe Louis Arena jubilation, a deep-throated "LUUUC!"

Sitting in Section 212A, Row 12, Seat 2, was Hull.

"That certainly makes it pretty special," Robitaille said. "It's going

TURN LEFT

Most goals by a left wing

PLAYER	GOALS	SEASONS
Luc Robitaille *	620	16
Bobby Hull	610	16
Dave Andreychuk *	593	20
Johnny Bucyk	556	23
Michel Goulet	548	15

* active player

to be meaningful once I retire, but I don't want to stop here. I want to keep going and win a Cup."

Later in the game, Bobby's son Brett scored what proved to be the winner, and it was the 99th of Brett's career, passing Bobby into third on the all-time list, behind Gordie Howe (121) and Phil Esposito (118).

With about two minutes left, Bobby left his seat and headed down the steps. The surrounding fans cheered. Bobby smiled. He held a forefinger to his lips, as if to

say, "Shhh," it wasn't his night.

He made his way to the dressing room.

"What are records for?" he asked.

"To be broken," a reporter said.

"Thank you," he said.

Robitaille asked Bobby to pose for a picture. He told him his first pair of skates was a Bobby Hull CCM model. Robitaille, in a sweaty gray T-shirt, clenched a cigar in his smile and the puck in his hand, 611 written in black marker on white tape stuck to the rubber. Bobby, in a dark overcoat, held Robitaille's 610 puck.

Bobby gave Robitaille that cigar — and laughed because Brett had given it to him for Christmas.

"So if Luc gets the cigar," a reporter asked, "what's Brett get?"

"Well," Bobby said, "he gets my love."

A SEASON OF MILESTONES

DIANE WEISS

Dominik Hasek continued to add to his impressive resume when he earned his 60th career shutout on Feb. 13.

Assist: Larionov

JULIAN H. GONZALEZ

Bob Ray and cat Wild Thing were among the beneficiaries of alert neighbor Igor Larionov. The Red Wings center awoke the sleeping Rays and their pets as their house burned late on the night of Jan. 20.

BY NICHOLAS J. COTSONIKA

To Bob and Suzanne Ray of Birmingham, not to mention their three cats, Igor Larionov is more than a member of the Red Wings.

He's a lifesaver.

"He literally saved our lives and our house," Bob Ray said.

Larionov arrived home late on a Sunday night, Jan. 20, after playing in the Wings' 3-2 overtime victory against Ottawa. Soon afterward, he and his wife, Elena, smelled something strange.

Smoke.

The Rays' house next door was on fire.

Larionov ran out, ran to their front door, screamed, banged, rang the bell. And he woke up the Rays. They had no idea.

Bob and Suzanne had been sound asleep with their cats: Wild Thing, Alley Cat and Snickers. Their bedroom was in the back of their ranch home, and the fire had ignited in the garage, where Ray had disposed of fireplace ashes he hadn't realized were still hot.

"Mr. Ray and his wife are very lucky people," said Tim Wangler, Birmingham assistant chief fire marshal.

The Larionovs called 911 at 12:31 a.m. The flashing lights came, and the fire was out in 20-30 minutes. Just in time. It had started to spread from the garage to the attic, where it could have spread quickly through the whole house.

"If it had been 15 minutes later, we wouldn't have had a house," Bob Ray said. "We're very fortunate."

Left outside in his underwear, shoeless and in the snow, Ray had nowhere to go. He and his wife couldn't return to their house. So the Larionovs brought the Rays into their house. Clothed them. Served them tea. Kept them company until almost dawn, when they left to stay with a relative.

"They were very hospitable," said Wangler, who interviewed the Rays at the Larionovs'. "It's the way it should be: neighbors helping neighbors." Larionov declined to comment on the incident. Wings spokesman John Hahn said Larionov played down his actions, saying, "Anybody would've done it," and he was glad he was in the right place at the right time.

Nevertheless, Wangler said: "He was instrumental in saving their lives, getting them out. It was one of those happy outcomes. You hate to see the fire: It was devastating to the Rays. But it could have been so much worse."

The season in review

OCTOBER

OCT. 4 — WINGS 4, SAN JOSE 3 (OT): Brendan Shanahan completes a hat trick with the overtime winner in the opener at San Jose. Brett Hull also scores his first goal as a Wing.

OCT. 10 — CALGARY 4, WINGS 2: The Wings lose their home opener, their first regular-season loss at Joe Louis Arena since Dec. 27, 2000, a streak of 19 games. Brendan Shanahan scores his league-leading fifth goal.

OCT. 12 — WINGS 4, BUFFALO 2: Dominik Hasek gets the best of his former team, making 29 saves at home. Nicklas Lidstrom records his 570th and 571st career points, passing Reed Larson as first all-time among Wings defensemen.

OCT. 13 — WINGS 5, N.Y. ISLANDERS 4 (OT): Steve Yzerman scores twice, including the winner 2:32 into overtime, on the road. Former Wings goalie Chris Osgood loses his first game of the season, stopping 28 shots.

OCT. 18 — WINGS 3, PHILADELPHIA 2: Sergei Fedorov scores at 19:19 of the third period to tie the game at 2, and Brett Hull's shot over the shoulder of goaltender Brian Boucher wins it with 17 seconds remaining at Joe Louis Arena.

OCT. 20 — WINGS 3, LOS ANGELES 2: Luc Robitaille scores the winner against his former team with 4:19 left in the second period at Detroit. Scotty Bowman becomes the first NHL coach to record 1,200 wins.

OCT. 27 — WINGS 1, NASHVILLE 0: Goaltender Manny Legace makes 15 saves, but leaves on a stretcher late in the second period after colliding with a pair of players. He spends the night in a Nashville hospital for precautionary neck X rays, but is fine.

OCT. 31 — WINGS 4, DALLAS 3 (OT): Happy Hulloween: Brett Hull notches two goals and an assist in his first game at Dallas since leaving as a free agent. He wins the game with a shot between Ed Belfour's legs 48 seconds into overtime.

NOVEMBER

NOV. 2 — WINGS 2, N.Y. ISLANDERS 1: With their wives sitting together in the stands, Kris Draper scores twice on former roommate Chris Osgood, making his first appearance at the Joe since the Islanders acquired him in the waiver draft.

NOV. 4 — CHICAGO 5, WINGS 4: Detroit scores three unanswered goals after trailing, 5-1, but loses its first game on the road. Dominik Hasek is pulled at 11:14 of the second period after giving up five goals on 14 shots.

NOV. 9 — WINGS 1, ANAHEIM 0: Luc Robitaille

Julie Draper, right, wife of Red Wing Kris Draper, and Jenna Osgood, wife of New York Islander Chris Osgood, a former Detroit goalie, had a good laugh before the game at Joe Louis Arena on Nov. 2.

JULIAN H. GONZALEZ

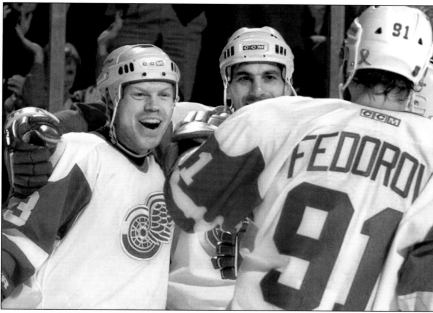

JULIAN H. GONZALEZ

Later, it was Draper's turn to laugh, as he celebrated his first-period goal against Osgood with Sergei Fedorov and Chris Chelios. Draper would score both goals against his former roommate in the 2-1 victory.

scores the winner in Anaheim, redirecting a wrist shot by Brendan Shanahan, and becomes the 13th NHL player with 600 career goals. The shutout is Dominik Hasek's first of the season.

NOV. 21 — WINGS 1, COLUMBUS 0 (OT): Manny Legace makes 38 saves, and Luc Robitaille's goal with 42.4 seconds left in overtime seals the shutout in Columbus.

NOV. 25 — WINGS 4, CHICAGO 4: After taking a 3-0 lead in the second period at home, the Wings fall behind, 4-3, before Darren McCarty's goal with 6:40 left salvages the tie.

NOV. 30 — WINGS 4, NEW JERSEY 2: Host Detroit improves to 8-0-1 in its past nine games. Sergei Fedorov and Igor Larionov each have a goal and an assist.

DECEMBER

DEC. 1 — NEW JERSEY 4, WINGS 1: The Wings' nine-game unbeaten streak ends in New Jersey.

DEC. 5 — COLORADO 4, WINGS 1: The defending Stanley Cup champions beat host Detroit, which loses back-to-back games for the first time all season. Sergei Fedorov beats Patrick

KIRTHMON F. DOZIER

Red Wing Sean Avery got into it with Edmonton's Scott Ferguson on March 13. Later, Chris Chelios scored the first regular-season overtime goal of his 19-year career, giving Detroit a 4-3 victory.

Roy with a backhander for the Wings' goal.

DEC. 10 — CALGARY 2, WINGS 0: The Wings extend their winless streak to four games, their longest drought since 0-3-2 on Jan. 11-19, 2000. Former Wings goalie Mike Vernon snaps his 13-game winless streak with the victory, making 28 saves in Calgary.

DEC. 17 — CHICAGO 2, WINGS 0: Manny Legace makes 35 saves at the Joe, including 19 in the second period, but loses for the first time in 20 decisions, dating to Dec. 27, 2000. The host Wings are 1-5-1 in their past seven.

DEC. 29 — NASHVILLE 3, WINGS 2 (OT): Former Michigan player Bubba Berenzweig scores at 2:20 of overtime and has two assists for the host Predators. The Wings had a 2-0 lead with less than five minutes remaining.

JANUARY

JAN. 5 — WINGS 3, COLORADO 1: Igor Larionov and Brendan Shanahan score less than two minutes apart early in the third period and extend the Wings' home unbeaten streak to six games. Dominik Hasek makes 13 saves; Colorado backup goaltender David Aebischer fills in for an ill Patrick Roy and faces 35 shots.

JAN. 9 — WINGS 5, VANCOUVER 4 (OT): Kris Draper's goal at 2:26 of overtime caps host Detroit's rally from a three-goal, third-period deficit. Luc Robitaille scores career goal No. 610, tying him with Bobby Hull for most goals by an NHL left wing.

JAN. 12 — WINGS 5, DALLAS 2: Brendan Shanahan reaches 1,000 career points with a goal 2:39 into the first period, then picks up another goal and an assist for good measure at Joe Louis Arena.

JAN. 18 — WINGS 3, WASHINGTON 1: With Bobby Hull sitting in the stands at the Joe,

A SEASON OF MILESTONES

JULIAN H. GONZALEZ

On March 28, Kris Draper found himself surrounded by a pack of Predators — goalie Tomas Vokoun, Vladimir Orszagh, and Denis Arkhipov, right. The game ended in a tie at 3, and the Wings clinched the Presidents' Trophy.

Luc Robitaille breaks his record for most goals by an NHL left wing, scoring No. 611 at 1:50 of the first period. The winner comes from Brett Hull — his 99th.

JAN. 20 — WINGS 3, OTTAWA 2: Steve Yzerman becomes the ninth NHL player with 1,000 assists, doing so on Mathieu Dandenault's winner 59 seconds into overtime at home.

JAN. 26 — WINGS 5, ST. LOUIS 2: Brett Hull caps a hat trick with an empty-netter at 19:33 of the third period in St. Louis. He also has two assists. The hat trick was the 31st of his career.

FEBRUARY

FEB. 4 — WINGS 3, COLORADO 1: The Grind Line powers Detroit's win in Denver, with goals by Darren McCarty and Kirk Maltby. Nicklas Lidstrom finishes the scoring with an empty-netter in the final two seconds.

FEB. 8 — COLUMBUS 3, WINGS 2: David Vyborny's goal 19 seconds into the third period ends Detroit's home win streak at 13 games.

FEB. 9 — WINGS 3, OTTAWA 2: Sergei Fedorov scores career goals 350 and 351 at Ottawa, and Steve Duchesne scores on the power play in Ottawa.

FEB. 11 — WINGS 3, MONTREAL 2: Steve Yzerman returns after missing six games following knee surgery. Brendan Shanahan ensures the win in Montreal with his 30th goal of the season, banking a shot off goaltender Jose Theodore at 19:46 of the third period.

FEB. 13 — WINGS 2, MINNESOTA 0: Dominik Hasek's fourth shutout of the season and 60th of his career sends the visiting Wings into the Olympic break with a victory.

FEB. 26 — WINGS 4, TAMPA BAY 3 (OT): In their first game since the Olympic break, the Wings win in Tampa thanks to Brendan Shanahan. Playing with a broken thumb, he scores two goals, including the winner.

FEB. 27 — WINGS 3, FLORIDA 2 (OT): Florida goaltender Roberto Luongo stops 57 shots, but it's the 60th of the game — by Brett Hull — that eludes him with 48.5 seconds left in overtime at Sunrise, Fla.

MARCH

MARCH 9 — WINGS 5, ST. LOUIS 2: The Wings reach 100 points for the season with their eighth straight win on the road, a team record. Hasek extends his unbeaten streak to 15 games, a career best.

MARCH 10 — BUFFALO 5, WINGS 1: In his first return to Buffalo since being traded by the Sabres, Hasek is pulled after allowing four goals on 22 shots. The loss is the Wings' most lopsided of the season.

MARCH 13 — WINGS 4, EDMONTON 3 (OT): Chris Chelios scores in Detroit on a one-timer with one minute left in overtime, his first regular-season overtime goal in a 19-year career.

MARCH 23 — WINGS 2, COLORADO 0: Brendan Shanahan breaks a tie in Denver at 7:48 of the third period with his 500th career goal. Brett Hull scores later in the period, and Dominik Hasek makes 31 saves in his 61st career shutout, best among active goaltenders.

MARCH 28 — WINGS 3, NASHVILLE 3: The host Wings pick up a point and clinch their third Presidents' Trophy in eight years as the NHL's top regular-season team.

APRIL

APRIL 10 — WINGS 3, CHICAGO 3: Steve Yzerman returns after missing 19 games with a knee injury. Darren McCarty scores career goal No. 100 with 5:03 left to tie the game for host Detroit.

APRIL 14 — ST. LOUIS 5, WINGS 3: The Wings end the regular season in Detroit with a loss — and in a 1-3-4-2 slump.

A SEASON OF MILESTONES

1-3-4-2

JULIAN H. GONZALEZ

Bottles and other debris replaced end-of-season octopi at Joe Louis Arena as fans vented their frustration with the referees — and perhaps with the Red Wings — as Detroit finished the regular season with a 5-3 loss to St. Louis.

BY NICHOLAS J. COTSONIKA

A brilliant regular season came to an ugly end.

The Red Wings finished with 116 points, 15 more than the NHL's next-best team, Boston, and second most in franchise history. But they lost to St. Louis, 5-3. Angry at the referees near game's end, fans threw bottles, cups and other garbage onto the Joe Louis Arena ice instead of the traditional April octopi.

The Wings would open the playoffs against Vancouver in a 1-3-4-2 slump.

"Obviously," Chris Chelios said, "defensively we were horrible the last 10 games — no one paying attention, no one doing their job, sometimes a lack of effort, sometimes a lack of thinking.

It's not one or two guys. It's the whole team. You don't mind losing. It's how you lose. And this is embarrassing."

The Presidents' Trophy had been secured March 28 — 2½ weeks before the season ended — so the Wings set their sights on the Stanley Cup, resting players to take care of fatigue and nagging injuries. They figured their intensity and continuity would suffer short-term, but they were willing to bet they would benefit long-term.

"We've said it all along: The regular season is the regular season — the playoffs are the playoffs," Scotty Bowman said. The Wings once entered the playoffs 7-7-6 and won the Cup (1997), and they entered 20-4-5 and lost in the first round (in 2001 to Los Angeles).

"We've done it every which way over the last few years," Bowman said. "We were determined to make sure our injured guys got over their injuries. I think we did that. Sure, you're going to lose some games because of it, and that's what you have to do. You weigh both sides."

Asked if the slump mattered, Chelios said, "We'll see.

"Yeah, it would have been great if we had come out with some momentum from this game, but we didn't, and it's in the past. Now we've got to go out and play great playoff hockey. For the first three quarters of the season, we played great. We've got to get back to that level, and we can if we want to do it. We've got a group of veterans here, and we've got to bear down."

A SEASON OF MILESTONES

MANDI WRIGHT

Olympic Interlude

Bring on the Canadians

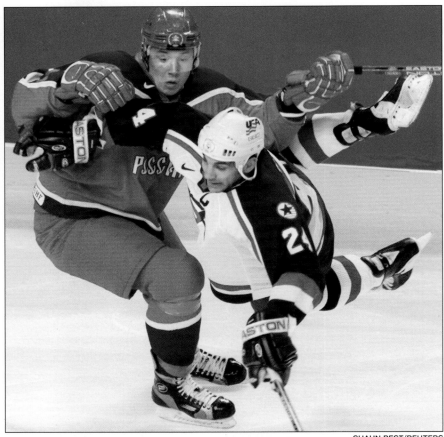

SHAUN BEST/REUTERS

U.S. captain Chris Chelios was sent flying by this collision with Russia's Ilya Kovalchuk, but the Americans' 3-2 victory put them in the gold-medal game — and sent Russia to a battle for bronze with Belarus.

BY NICHOLAS J. COTSONIKA

WEST VALLEY CITY, Utah — The puck dropped, the final second ticked away and, like little boys, the Americans mobbed each other around goaltender Mike Richter. They had survived. The Russians mounted a frantic comeback attempt in the third period of the men's hockey semifinals, but the Americans held on for a 3-2 victory, and they will go for gold against Canada.

"It's almost too good to be true," U.S. captain Chris Chelios said.

Bill Guerin, Scott Young and Phil Housley scored rebound power-play goals for the Americans. Then Alexei Kovalev and Vladimir Malakhov scored early in the third period for the Russians, and the teams made a mad dash to the end.

On the 22nd anniversary of the "Miracle on Ice" — the shocking U.S. upset of the Soviet Union at Lake Placid — the Americans and Russians were magnificent on ice. They skated. They scored. With speed and skill and savvy, they played some of the most entertaining hockey you'll ever see.

"That third period was an onslaught of some of the best talent in the world at the highest pace possible," U.S. forward Jeremy Roenick said. "My heart was in my stomach for the whole third period. I almost threw up."

Wings center Sergei Fedorov had a dangerous chance for Russia about 12:23 into the first period. He split two defensemen, Housley and Dearborn native Brian Rafalski, and stepped in on Richter. But he fired the puck low into Richter's pads.

"I think we went out and thought, 'Maybe it's just going to happen for us and they're going to roll over,' and they didn't," said the Americans' Brett Hull. "They're a great team, and they came back at us, and we had to play our asses off to win."

Bring on the Americans

BY NICHOLAS J. COTSONIKA

WEST VALLEY CITY, Utah — Steve Yzerman couldn't help himself. He rifled a wrist shot into the net, kicking off Canada's 7-1 blowout of Belarus in the men's hockey semifinals, and he didn't stay stoic as he usually does when he scores for the Red Wings. He pumped his left fist. Not once. But twice.

"I'm trying to stay calm," Yzerman said. "I don't like getting really fired up because I think you get up there and then there's a crash a lot of times. I try to contain my emotions as much as I can. But it's pretty hard. You're pretty fired up."

How can any Canadian contain his emotions? Hockey isn't the national pastime. It's the national passion. The Canadian women's team upset the United States and won its first Olympic gold medal in the Games. Now the men's team will go against the Americans for its first gold in half a century. Televisions will be tuned in from coast to coast.

"The streets are going to be pretty empty," said Canada's Brendan Shanahan, "unless you've got a car with a satellite dish on it."

The Belarussians had only one NHL player, Anaheim's Ruslan Salei. But in the quarterfinals they had beaten Sweden in the biggest Olympic hockey upset since the United States shocked the Soviet Union in 1980 at Lake Placid.

Shanahan didn't play much for what coach Pat Quinn said were "medical reasons," but he assisted on the final goal, earning his first point of the Olympic tournament. Yzerman added two assists and finished with three points against Belarus.

"Steve is marvelous," Quinn said. "I always knew he was a great player, but he's more. He's a walking example of the things you need to do to be successful. He cares about himself. He's got great self-respect, and when that self-respect comes through, it affects other people."

Yzerman had arthroscopic surgery on his right knee Jan. 28. Concerned, Quinn and executive director Wayne Gretzky asked Yzerman to disqualify himself from the Salt Lake Games if he felt he wouldn't

PETER POWER/ASSOCIATED PRESS

Canadian captain Mario Lemieux, right, and teammate Steve Yzerman embraced after their 7-1 Olympic semifinal victory over Belarus, as Canadian fans celebrated with an outburst of flag-waving.

be able to contribute. Canada had several good players in reserve to replace him, with Joe Thornton at the top of the list.

"With a guy like Steve, you almost sometimes have to jump in and say, 'Hey, you can't do it. Get out of the way,'" Quinn said. "But it was his call."

In Canada's third game, against the Czechs, Quinn put Yzerman on the top line with Paul Kariya and Mario Lemieux. "I didn't expect it," Yzerman said. "I was like, 'Whoa. I'm going to try to take advantage of this.'

"I'm enjoying playing," Yzerman said. "The last Olympics was a ton of fun. This will probably be the last one for me. I don't know that I'll be playing in four years. Just trying to make the most of the opportunity.

"Canada wants the gold medal, and the people will be disappointed if we don't get it. I just really want to win."

TALE OF TAPE: U.S. VS. CANADA

WE'RE: Red, White and Blue.

THEY'RE: Red, White and Labatt's Blue.

WE HAVE: 34 medals at Salt Lake, including 10 gold.

THEY HAVE: 17 medals at Salt Lake, including six gold (counting that belated tie in pairs figure skating).

WE SWEPT: Men's snowboarding halfpipe.

THEY SWEEP: With curling brooms.

THEY INVENTED: Hockey and Don Cherry.

WE INVENTED: The Zamboni, TV time-outs, the glow puck and the Mighty Ducks of Anaheim.

WE HAVE: Two Red Wings, Brett Hull and Chris Chelios (the Captain).

THEY HAVE: Two Red Wings, Brendan Shanahan and Steve Yzerman (the Alternate Captain).

WE HAVE: An 8-1 win over Belarus.

THEY HAVE: A 7-1 win over Belarus.

THEY LAST WON: Gold in 1952.

WE LAST WON: Gold in 1980, the Miracle on Ice. Which is when Canada decided to take the Olympics seriously again.

WE WERE PLAYING: To erase Nagano memories of trashed dorm rooms.

THEY WERE PLAYING: To erase Nagano memories of Dominik Hasek.

Worth the wait

BY NICHOLAS J. COTSONIKA

WEST VALLEY CITY, Utah — As the clock counted down on Canada's 5-2 victory over the United States, Canadian fans broke out in song. And not just any song. They sang "O Canada" loud and proud. "God keep our land glorious and free."

"It gave us chills," said Canada's Brendan Shanahan.

Then the buzzer sounded and it was over — the game, the tournament, the torment. As coach Pat Quinn said, Canadians feel they invented hockey, developed hockey, taught hockey to the world. Now they had the Olympic men's hockey gold medal. For the first time in half a century.

"It's a huge victory," said Canada's Steve Yzerman. "Hockey, it's the No. 1 sport in Canada, the most popular sport. So we're thrilled to be Olympic champions."

While the Canadians celebrated, the Americans watched. They had failed to finish the fairy tale. The Salt Lake Games opened with the 1980 hockey team lighting the Olympic cauldron. Here they could have ended with the 2002 team winning gold, 22 years to the day after the '80 team did, led by the same coach, Herb Brooks.

When it was over, captain Chris Chelios led the team to center ice. The players raised their sticks to the crowd in unison, and the American fans cheered. In a sense, they hadn't lost gold as much as they had won silver. The medal was the United States' first in men's hockey since 1980.

While the Americans played well from the start at Salt Lake, the Canadians struggled early, losing to Sweden, 5-2, in their first game and beating Germany, 3-2, in their second. Things got so bad

MIKE BLAKE/REUTERS

Jarome Iginla's second goal of the gold-medal game gave Canada a 4-2 lead and levitated Steve Yzerman into Iginla's arms behind Team USA's Brian Rafalski.

that executive director Wayne Gretzky, normally reserved, lashed out at everyone from critics to fans to officials in a news conference.

But the Canadians came into their own in the gold-medal game. They finished with only a 39-33 advantage in shots, but they had a decided advantage in the play most of the day. Had they not hit

posts and crossbars, had U.S. goaltender Mike Richter not been so sharp, they might have won by a larger margin.

"We won convincingly," Canada's Michael Peca said. "It was great to see."

The Americans' Tony Amonte opened the scoring 8:49 into the first period. Paul Kariya tied the score at 14:50, and at 18:33 Jarome

Iginla put Canada ahead, 2-1. Dearborn native Brian Rafalski tied it on the power play 15:30 into the second, with Brett Hull earning an assist, but that was all for the Americans.

Joe Sakic gave the Canadians a 3-2 lead on the power play at 18:19, and the goal would prove to be the winner. Iginla scored again at 16:01 into the third. Yzerman, who earned an assist on the play, leapt with joy on the ice. Gretzky went crazy in the stands. At 18:40, Sakic iced it. He broke in on Richter and beat his right pad. Shanahan jumped on top of Sakic in a pile along the boards. Yzerman jumped to his feet on the bench and hugged a couple of teammates. The fans started singing the anthem.

"True patriot love. . . ."

"It's unbelievable," Shanahan said. "It was a historic game for both countries. The USA team has nothing to be ashamed of. They played great. We broke it open at the end, but it was a tight game throughout."

The teams lined up and shook hands. Shanahan and Yzerman hugged Chelios and Hull. The Americans congratulated the Canadians. The Canadians consoled the Americans.

"You know, it doesn't prove that Canada's the best," Yzerman said. "We're just Olympic champions, that's all."

The Americans received their silver medals. Chelios frowned after his went around his neck. Hull winked and sort of smiled. Then the Canadians received their gold medals. As soon as his went around his neck, Shanahan looked down, took it in his left hand and examined it.

"It's nice and heavy," he said. Then he stepped back, waved to his family in the stands and held it up. "My mother, my brother and his two kids," he said. "My American wife (Catherine) who was cheering for Canada."

Four years earlier, in the semifinals at Nagano — the first Olympics to include NHL players — Canada lost to the Czech Republic

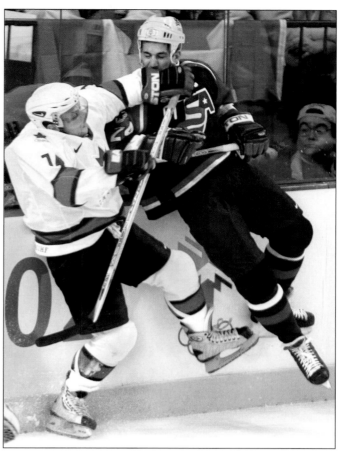

ERICH SCHLEGEL/DALLAS MORNING NEWS

U.S. captain Chris Chelios got what he wanted, "a Canada-USA final," though he probably could have done without this check by Canada's Theo Fleury.

PHOTO NEXT PAGE BY DAVID P. GILKEY

After "O Canada" was played, the gold-medal game's Red Wing contingent — from left, Steve Yzerman, Chris Chelios, Brett Hull and Brendan Shanahan — gathered to display their gold and silver medals.

in a shoot-out. Shanahan was the last man Dominik Hasek stoned, and Shanahan said then that he had let down his country.

"Nagano was such a disappointment," Shanahan said. "When I wasn't initially invited to try out for the (2002) team, I just thought, 'Well, I guess that's it for my Olympic experience.' So to be sitting here today with a gold medal, I feel like a pretty lucky man."

Yzerman grabbed Owen Nolan's video camera and taped Nolan receiving his medal, then he gave it back and received his medal with a big smile. Early in his career, Yzerman was cut from Canada Cup teams. He thought Nagano might have been his last shot at Olympic glory. Now he was a national hero more than ever.

"It's a great moment," he said. After the Canadian anthem was played, Shanahan and Yzerman took a picture on the ice with Chelios and Hull.

"We talked about it before the tournament, thinking this was what North America wanted, a Canada-USA final," Chelios said. "And then, when it got to be that, we didn't know if we really wanted that. It was wild, the look we gave each other in the cafeteria" at the Olympic Village.

Chelios said he meant no disrespect toward the other Wings who played at the Olympics. Pavel Datsyuk, Sergei Fedorov and Igor Larionov won bronze for Russia. Nicklas Lidstrom, Tomas Holmstrom and Fredrik Olausson lost with Sweden in the quarterfinals, as Hasek did with the Czechs.

But, Chelios said, he had a special bond with Shanahan and Yzerman, a "North American thing."

"Shanny and Stevie, I've been growing up with them guys," Chelios said. "I've been through the wars with those guys. I'm proud of those guys. I'm happy for them. I'm happy for us, and I'm just as happy for them."

JULIAN H. GONZALEZ

The Playoffs

All or nothing

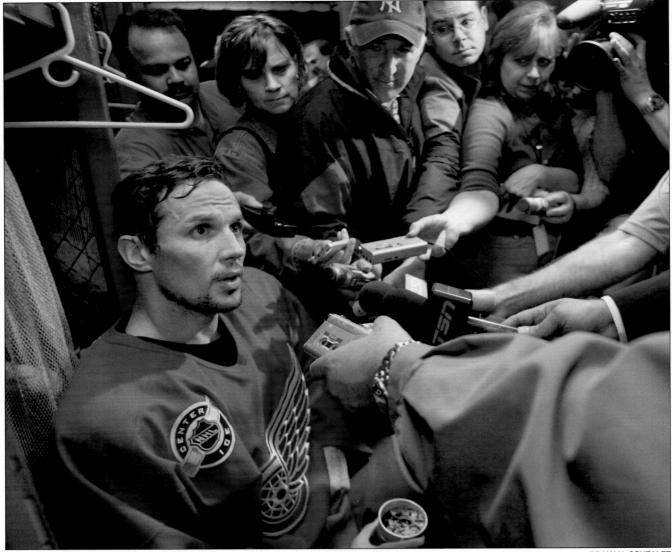

JULIAN H. GONZALEZ

After a great regular season and facing the first-round series with Vancouver, captain Steve Yzerman and his teammates had one thing to say: We want the Cup.

BY NICHOLAS J. COTSONIKA

When Luc Robitaille signed in the summer of 2001, he knew what he was getting into: If the Red Wings make the Stanley Cup finals, and they go to a seventh game, and they go to a third overtime, and the puck takes a bad bounce into their net . . . "It's not a good year," Robitaille said.

Great regular season? So what? We want the Cup.

On the eve of the playoffs, the stakes were higher than ever. With Hall of Famer Scotty Bowman coaching nine potential Hall of Famers, the Wings were chasing more than a third Cup in six seasons. They could take their place among the most memorable teams of all time, if not a spot among the greatest.

"It's a special opportunity," Robitaille said.

Think of how this run would affect the prestige and pocketbook of owner Mike Ilitch. His Tigers were toothless. He took heat for not living up to a promise to spend on them. But his Wings were winners, and after saying he would do "whatever's necessary" to keep them in Cup contention after the 2000-01 season, he spent, spent, spent, acquiring Robitaille, Dominik Hasek and Brett Hull, raising his payroll to about $65 million.

THE PLAYOFFS

JULIAN H.GONZALEZ

For Brett Hull and the Red Wings' high-priced, veteran talent, a Stanley Cup was the only acceptable goal.

"I thought we had a great team before," forward Brendan Shanahan said. "I think we have a better team now."

But there were worries. Senior vice president Jimmy Devellano had said the Wings would not turn a profit unless they had "a heck of a run" in the playoffs.

General manager Ken Holland was in a tough spot. If the Wings won, he would have his second Cup as GM, but people might say he bought it with Ilitch's money. If they lost, people might say he didn't spend the money wisely and the Wings were too old.

After falling short three straight years, Bowman finally followed up with Cups in 1997 and 1998. Then he fell short three straight years once more. Win and he would have his ninth Cup as a coach — one more than his mentor, Toe Blake. Lose and his legacy could be questioned.

Yzerman had an injured right knee but opted to play in the Olympics. But if he were to raise the Cup, people wouldn't question how he came back quickly from surgery, pushed the knee while winning a gold medal for Canada, aggravated it and sat out all but one game for the rest of the regular season.

Hasek didn't even want to think about it. He had six Vezina trophies as the NHL's best goaltender and two Hart trophies as its most valuable player, but he had never won the Cup, let alone the Conn Smythe Trophy as playoff MVP. His rival, Patrick Roy, had won three Vezinas and no Harts but four Cups and three Conn Smythes. With Hasek's future uncertain, he wanted the Cup and he wanted it now.

"This is why I asked to be trad-ed to Detroit, to a team which has a chance to win the Cup," Hasek said. "And here we are. I'm very excited about it."

Robitaille hadn't won the Cup, either. Neither had defenseman Steve Duchesne, a 16-year veteran who stuck around even when the Wings didn't appear to want him at one point. Chelios, 40, hadn't won the Cup since 1985-86, when he was with Montreal.

"You don't get many opportunities like this," Chelios said. "I don't take it for granted. I know I've got to go out and have a great playoff. Not knowing what's in the future, I've just got to go out and hope this is our year."

"If everyone does their job," Hull said, "we should be fine.

"It doesn't always work out the way you plan." On the other hand, he added with a smile, "sometimes it does."

'They got lucky'

BY NICHOLAS J. COTSONIKA

ERIC SEALS

Vancouver's overtime victory in Game I was a much happier occasion for Canucks Jan Hlavac and Trevor Linden (16) than for Dominik Hasek.

The payroll, the potential Hall of Famers, everything the Red Wings had going for them in their all-or-nothing quest for the Stanley Cup could be wiped out by mistakes and bad breaks. And as several Wings said after losing the playoff opener to Vancouver in overtime, 4-3, "That's playoff hockey."

The Wings hit a crossbar and a post. The Canucks got two goals when shots went in off Wings, including the winner. Henrik Sedin fired from the top of the right circle. The puck banked off Igor Larionov and past the left shoulder of goaltender Dominik Hasek at 13:59.

"They got lucky," Hasek said. "But it's part of the game."

The Wings took the lead three times. The dogged, underdog Canucks came back three times. The last time, Mathieu Dandenault tried to pass out of his zone in traffic instead of banking the puck off the boards. The puck hit a shin pad. It stayed in. With 9:13 left in regulation, Trevor Linden scored.

"I didn't get it out," Dandenault said. "If I make the safe play there. ... The puck's got to get out. That's the bottom line."

Luc Robitaille, Sergei Fedorov and Larionov scored for the Wings. Todd Warriner and Andrew Cassels also scored for the Canucks. The loss was the Wings' fifth straight in the playoffs, dating to their 2001 series against the Kings.

Steve Yzerman, on a sore right knee, played his 155th playoff game for the Wings, breaking Gordie Howe's record.

Despite the victory, Vancouver center Brendan Morrison wasn't ready to celebrate. "If there's any team in the league that has a switch they can turn on and off," he said, "it's this team right here."

OCTOMETER

A few observations on the NHL playoffs (rated on a scale of one to four octopi):

 It seems kind of early for a must-win game, doesn't it? But you have to figure the Wings better stop this snowball while they can.

 Times like these, though, are when the great ones like Hasek are not only supposed to get mad, they're supposed to get even. As in following a so-so performance with a dominating one.

 The Canucks, by the way, ought to show a little more respect to Chris Chelios. Age before Bertuzzi.

Code red

BY MITCH ALBOM

Get out of town. Change the scenery. Change the view. Go to Canada. Western Canada. Far western Canada. Anywhere but here, Detroit, Joe Louis Arena, where the only thing the Red Wings have is bad karma, two quixotic playoff losses, a memory reel of clanged posts, missed chances, intercepted passes, fluttering pucks and questions, questions, questions.

How is this happening? Where is your goalie? Where is your power play? Vancouver again, 5-2? Who are these guys? Who are you guys?

Get out of town.

In 48 hours, the Wings went from top gun to pop gun, home-ice advantage to road-ice disadvantage, a Stanley Cup favorite to down, two games to none, in the first round. They've lost their bite. They've lost their magic.

The home fans were periodically booing in Game 2 — when they weren't screaming "SHOOT THE PUCK!" — and the biggest import of the off-season was looking like a lemon. Dominik Hasek, the miracle goalie, did not deliver.

The Canucks had three goals on their first 10 shots and five on 20 by the end. Sorry. That's not why you pay $8 million a year. Two of those pucks should have been stopped, including the crushing fourth goal, which effectively ended the game. It came on a Markus Naslund shot late in the third period, a shot that wasn't screened, wasn't tipped, wasn't anything, a shot Hasek stops in practice.

Todd Bertuzzi, Andrew Cassels, Scott Lachance and Matt Cooke also scored for the Canucks. Nicklas Lidstrom and Steve

KIRTHMON F. DOZIER

Facing an 0-2 deficit didn't sit well with coach Scotty Bowman after Vancouver's 5-2 victory at Joe Louis Arena.

Yzerman scored for the Wings.

"I didn't play well," Hasek said. "No excuses."

Meanwhile, Vancouver's goalie, a 25-year-old named Dan Cloutier who was playing in the fourth playoff game of his career, stymied the Wings' Hall of Fame scorers with astonishing ease.

"I always said the most dangerous teams to play were the ones who battled just to get into the playoffs," Yzerman said. "They've been playing playoff hockey for a

few weeks. We're sort of just getting started."

Yzerman was one of the few bright spots, scoring one goal, assisting on another, banging the Canucks and showing typical courage in fighting an obviously still painful knee injury.

"I'm not at all concerned about the goaltending," Yzerman said. "When this series is done, you're gonna say, 'It's unbelievable that Dominik Hasek, how well he's playing for Detroit.'"

A must win

BY NICHOLAS J. COTSONIKA

VANCOUVER, British Columbia — They cut down on their mistakes. They got the kind of breaks the Canucks did in Games 1 and 2. Dominik Hasek started to show some of the stuff expected of him — even stopping a penalty shot with 3:06 left.

The tide turned for the Red Wings, as they beat Vancouver, 3-1, and reduced their deficit in this first-round playoff series to 2-1.

"That was a do-or-die game," Brett Hull said. "I think it gives everybody a little confidence that in Game 4 if you go out and play well and win, the series is tied again."

The Wings' power play, which hadn't been effective, produced a goal by Steve Yzerman. The Canucks hit a post, and Nicklas Lidstrom scored what turned out to be the winner with a lucky long shot late in the second period.

Hasek made 22 saves, and his best were when they mattered most. With 9:06 left, he got his right arm on a sharp shot from the left circle by Markus Naslund. With 4:35 left, he scrambled to his left and robbed defenseman Ed Jovanovski.

Then, after Lidstrom broke up a breakaway for Todd Bertuzzi, who had scored earlier, Hasek closed his pads and stopped Bertuzzi from going five-hole on the penalty shot.

"I was nervous to be down, 2-0," Hasek said. "I was a little more nervous than usual. It was a must-win game for us. We've done our job."

KIRTHMON F. DOZIER

Nicklas Lidstrom earned pats aplenty for his blast from 90 feet that turned out to be the winning goal as the Red Wings cut Vancouver's lead to 2-1.

They say Hasek is one of five or six goaltenders who can win a game for you, Yzerman pointed out. "He maybe didn't win us the game, but he certainly preserved the win for us in the third," Yzerman said. "He's an experienced guy, been through a lot, and I don't think he's going to be fazed by the two losses that we had.

"There were some strange goals that went in on him. Everybody was kind of, 'What's wrong with Dom?' Or 'He's not playing his best.' But it's difficult for a goalie on redirections and deflections. You just hope you're in the right spot. Unfortunately in the

The Captain speaks

VANCOUVER, British Columbia — The Captain stood up in the dressing room before practice, and for three or four minutes he addressed his team.

The Red Wings had flown all night across the continent after losing the first two games of their first-round playoff series at Joe Louis Arena, where frustrated fans had voiced their dismay. They hadn't won in nine games, and their only victory in their past dozen was against Atlanta, the NHL's worst team.

Publicly, Steve Yzerman said only that "we just had a little brief meeting," and his teammates, knowing how Yzerman abhors their talking about him — wanting to preserve the code of The Room — weren't willing to give too many details.

But word leaked that Yzerman spoke calmly and directly, almost as if he were reading from a cue card, and he drove his message home. And that helped the Wings when they beat the Canucks in Game 3, 3-1.

"The veteran presence on our team is probably why we didn't panic," Brendan Shanahan said. "We came out with a very solid, controlled, calm, hardworking effort."

An Yzerman effort.

Asked what he told the team, Yzerman said, "I thought, despite losing the first two, we did a lot of good things. The thing we couldn't do was beat ourselves up. So again it was, 'Let's just relax. We'll be ready for the game. Go out and play hockey.' . . . At some point in the playoffs — unfortunately it was after two games — you're faced with a must-win game. It's how you respond in that one. Either you respond and play well, or you go home. Been through it before.

"So we're comfortable that, 'Hey, if we just win, we're all right, we're in good shape, it's not the end of the world.' Coming in here down, 2-zip, we felt pretty good about ourselves and our chances of winning this series."

Yzerman said his speech "wasn't anything brilliant," but Kris Draper said, "He's the kind of guy, when he steps up the whole room just listens. He picks his spots. That's why he's such a great leader. A guy can say things, but he goes out and backs everything up. When he speaks, it's great to hear him because of the way he goes out and plays hard."

By Nicholas J. Cotsonika

Bad sports

While the Wings were playing Vancouver, the Pistons were playing Toronto in a first-round NBA playoff series. Before Game I at the Palace, "O Canada" drew a stream of boos from some among the sold-out crowd — which included about a thousand Raptors fans waving Canadian flags. Later in the game, the crowd chanted, "USA! USA!"

Ugly Americans, eh?

"That was a little distasteful," the Pistons' Jerry Stackhouse said. "I don't think anyone enjoyed it. But our fans stuck up for us all season, so I'm going to stick up for them. I'm sure they were booing Toronto the team, not Canada the country."

Fair enough, but why were some Canadian fans booing in Vancouver during the "Star-Spangled Banner" before Game 3 of the Wings-Canucks? (And that was after the Canucks' orca mascot skated around GM Place with an octopus in its mouth, but that's OK — killer whales really do eat squids and stuff.)

Isn't it great how sports bring people together?

JULIAN H. GONZALEZ

Fans respected the singing of both national anthems and did not boo during Game 4 in Vancouver.

first two games, every deflection went right in the corner."

Asked whether he had done anything differently in Game 3, Hasek said: "I didn't do anything differently. I think overall we played a better game, and myself" — he smiled — "at least no bad bounces."

Even Steven

BY NICHOLAS J. COTSONIKA

VANCOUVER, British Columbia — Much changed after the Red Wings were booed off the ice at Joe Louis Arena, trailing their first-round playoff series, 2-0, winless in their previous nine games.

"The last month of the season, we definitely lost something," Steve Yzerman said. "And I feel we've regained it now."

The Wings were headed home after beating Vancouver, 4-2, and tying the series, 2-2. From Dominik Hasek to the Grind Line, the Wings found that missing desperation, cohesion and confidence.

"We're much sharper," Yzerman said. "We're into playoff hockey now."

Said Hasek: "It's a great feeling. We've done our job, and now we start from the beginning again."

"In the playoffs, if you want to win, each game you have to get better," associate coach Dave Lewis said. "You have to raise your level of everything: your intensity, your discipline, your skills, your passing, your grinding, your hits. We're getting better."

As much as the Wings had improved, the difference between the teams remained so slim that Yzerman illustrated it by gesturing with his left hand, his index finger an inch from his thumb. "It's been very close, and it's been excellent hockey," Yzerman said. "Both teams are getting better in the series, and it's made for better hockey with each game. ... I mean, it wasn't easy to win. We certainly got our share of breaks."

As the Canucks did in the first two games, the Wings scored lucky goals and took advantage of turnovers. The Wings took a

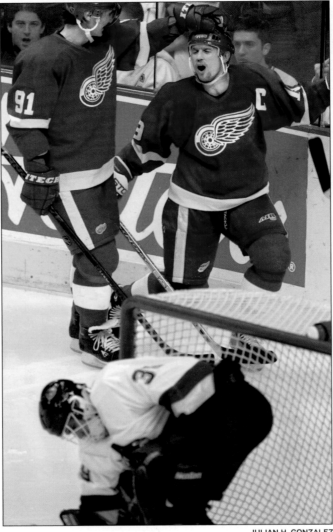

JULIAN H. GONZALEZ

By scoring the winning goal in Game 4, Steve Yzerman squared the first-round series at two wins apiece, and he earned a pat on the head from Sergei Fedorov. "We're into playoff hockey now," the Captain declared.

quick 2-0 lead as Jiri Fischer's goal went in off a Canuck and Chris Chelios' went in through traffic. Then the Wings sat back, didn't attack enough and allowed the Canucks to swarm them and tie the score at 2 in the second period.

Yzerman scored the winner by finishing a pretty play in the third, but it came on an ugly turnover by Vancouver defenseman Mattias Ohlund deep in his zone. Yzerman's seven points to that point in the series gave him 159 for his playoff career, one more than Gordie Howe.

A rejuvenated Wings team was headed home with the resolve to turn the boos of the home fans into cheers. Brendan Shanahan said, "We're really looking forward to playing in front of our fans and giving them a little bit better of a show than we gave them the first two games."

Captain Courageous

Iffy's lost weight recently, and friends have asked how he's done it. Iffy, they say, what's your body solution?

Simple, dear readers: A ladle of magical elixir (flavored with juniper berries and imported from Britain) in the evening (repeat as needed), and no eating three hours before bedtime. Of course Iffy savors his late-night snacks, so he's been up until dawn most days waiting for those three hours to elapse.

Good thing, too, because if he weren't up late, Iffy wouldn't have seen the Captain blaze his way into the record books while the Wings were playing in the middle of the night in Vancouver.

The Captain — we've been calling him that for 16 of his 19 seasons, so there's hardly any need to say his name — passed Gordie Howe in Red Wings playoff scoring in Game 4 at Vancouver. Their playoff numbers are remarkably similar: Gordie — 154 games, 67 goals, 91 assists, 158 points. The Captain — through 158 games, had 64 goals, 95 assists, 159 points.

Readers without gray hair might think of Howe as Mr. Hockey — a sobriquet Iffy's never gotten his arms around — or as the cuddly granddad in those car commercials. Iffy, more plainly, has long thought of Howe as the meanest and greatest player ever to sharpen his skates.

He could control a game like no other, loping down the ice, bullying into position, blistering a wrist shot past the goalie. Howe also could play defense and — like the Captain — he killed penalties.

But unlike the Captain, Howe

JULIAN H. GONZALEZ

Two heroes of a previous Detroit dynasty, Gordie Howe, left, and Ted Lindsay, presented the Stanley Cup to Steve Yzerman in 1997, after he led the Red Wings to their first Cup title in 42 years.

was the team's enforcer, and one night back in 1959 he nearly killed Rangers defenseman Lou Fontinato, who had been pestering him. (You see now why Iffy cannot warm up to the smarmy title of Mr. Hockey — Mr. Stay Out Of My Face Or I'll Bust Your Chops And Send You Back To Manitoba would be more like it.)

In Iffy's mind, Howe ranks right up there with Cobb, Jordan and Brown as the greatest to play their games. In hockey, Howe tops Gretzky and Orr hands-down and elbows-up.

But now, and without further ado, Iffy would like to add the Captain to his short list of hockey greats. Hitherto, Iffy had a deep regard for the Captain, but he thought of him as a second-10 kind of guy — y'know, not top 10 but second 10. No longer, and not sim-

ply because the Captain has bettered Gordie's numbers in the toughest season of them all — the second season — but because of the way the Captain has lifted his team (and on one knee, Iffy might add).

It wasn't long ago that office wags dubbed the Captain "Casper," as in Casper the Friendly Ghost, because he had a tendency to disappear during the playoffs. Now it's the Wings who would've disappeared had not the Captain rallied them to victory in Vancouver, and not once but twice.

That's why he has earned his place in Iffy's heart and Red Wings lore. And Iffy doesn't know what more you can ask of the Captain.

Of course, after delivering a third Cup, he could be called by his given name: Stevie Wonder.

Job well done

BY MITCH ALBOM

Brett Hull loped a shot into the crease, like a Little League coach throwing a grounder to his shortstop — and here came the shortstop, Sergei Fedorov, flying in and tapping the puck so deftly and quickly that by the time the red light flashed he was already circling away, hands in the air, rocking back on one skate like a man without a care in the world.

Nice job. Now finish it.

Game 5 may finally have been the happy rainstorm Red Wings fans dream of — four goals in the first period en route to a shutout victory — but it won't mean a thing if they ain't got that sting. Great teams take the fires of a victory like this and use them to burn the other guy's building.

Nice job. Now finish it.

"The last thing we want to do is take a breath and find ourselves in a Game 7," said Mathieu Dandenault, who scored in the Wings' 4-0 victory over Vancouver, their third straight on their way to a 3-2 playoff series lead. "Right now, Vancouver's probably down because they had a 2-0 lead on us. You don't want to give them anything to look forward to."

Remember, the Wings are not in these playoffs to prove they can beat the Canucks. They are in them to win a Cup. The less blood, sweat and pain exerted in this first-round series, the more they have for another.

"I think we found it tonight," Fedorov said. Found it and flaunted it.

That first period was a geyser, a burst dam, an exploding radiator on a smoking-hot highway. Goals were shooting out like balls from a tennis machine. Here was Tomas Holmstrom, on a power play, slap-

After Vancouver president and GM Brian Burke blasted the officiating prior to Game 5, the Red Wings sent him and the Canucks back home for Game 6 with the checklist completed.

JULIAN H. GONZALEZ

ping a long rebound off goalie Dan Cloutier right back at him: 1-0.

Here was Fedorov, the Wings shorthanded now, weaving through defenders, dishing off to Dandenault, who fired between Cloutier's legs: 2-0.

Here was Hull, with that wonderful leaning wrist shot — he looks as if he's posing for a trading card — and the shot again came off Cloutier and landed in front,

where Boyd Devereaux slapped it home with no resistance. Score: 3-0. And bye, bye, goalie.

Three minutes later, Fedorov did his shortstop thing against replacement goalie Peter Skudra, and that was that: 4-0.

This all happened, by the way, in a period in which the Wings were penalized three times to Vancouver's one. That should have caught the interest of one red-faced

Sergei Fedorov centered a troika of Red Wings — with Boyd Devereaux, left, and Chris Chelios — celebrating Fedorov's second goal of first period of Game 5 versus Vancouver.

gentleman in an upper-level seat, the president and general manager of the Canucks, Brian Burke.

For some unknown reason, in a news conference after Game 4, Burke went off on the Wings and the referees. He insisted that his team was getting terrible calls, that his players were being mugged, that Henrik Sedin was getting "his face washed" by a "scrum" of Detroit players, and that behemoth Todd Bertuzzi was "wearing three red sweaters" because the Wings were so busy tackling him.

He also accused Dominik Hasek of flopping like a fish and reminded officials that his goalie, Cloutier, was easy to identify because he was the one in pads, standing up. Actually, Brian, in Game 5, Cloutier was the one without a mask, sitting down. But why quibble over details?

What a difference a week makes, eh? Suddenly Hasek has a rhythm and was superb in stopping 25 shots. Fedorov is flying. Hull is finding ways to be precious without scoring. The defense is tightening, the penalty killing is sharp. And we needn't bother commenting on Steve Yzerman. He speaks for himself.

Nice job. Now finish it.

Fun finish

JULIAN H. GONZALEZ

From left, Chris Chelios, Kris Draper and Kirk Maltby were up in arms as the Red Wings closed out Vancouver.

BY NICHOLAS J. COTSONIKA

VANCOUVER, British Columbia — After the final horn and the handshakes, Chris Chelios skated to the Detroit bench. He smiled. He threw up his arms at the fans who had booed him like a villain.

Chelios and the Red Wings had the last laugh in this first-round series. After losing the first two games to the up-and-coming Ca-

nucks — at Joe Louis Arena, no less — they won four straight, finishing with a wild 6-4 victory.

Brett Hull had his first career playoff hat trick. Igor Larionov had a goal and three assists. Tomas Holmstrom and Nicklas Lidstrom also scored. Chelios had four assists.

"I'm glad we could win this series, because the Canucks just as easily could have beaten us," Hull said. "They are a fantastic

team, and the rest of the NHL should be wary of them. They're young. They're strong. They're fast. So they're going to be reckoned with in the future."

After failing to score earlier in the series, Hull had a good time.

"There's nothing more fun than scoring," he said.

Pause.

"Well, there's a couple things," he said, "but they're not involved in hockey."

Wings win: What a drag

SUSAN TUSA

When it came time to pay off his bet with mechanic Pete Melistas, left, Ray Kite didn't skirt the issue. He worked his shift in this little number, borrowed from the service station's bookkeeper, Marian Enright.

BY MICHAEL ROSENBERG

Ray Kite had to borrow a co-worker's clothes. Not a big deal, but the co-worker is named Marian, and these weren't blue jeans. Kite wore a dress to his job as a mechanic's assistant at Grosse Pointe Shell.

Kite, a Colorado Avalanche fan, bet another co-worker, Pete Melistas, that the Red Wings would lose their first-round series to the Vancouver Canucks. He made the bet after the Wings lost the first two games at home.

What kind of dress was it? A cocktail dress? An evening gown?

"A long black one," Kite said, in true Guy Mode. "It has a colored print all over it."

Kite, 20, also wore a sun hat, which really made the outfit. But he also wore his usual work boots, which was, like, totally gauche. "They wouldn't let me wear heels because it was too dangerous," he said.

Sounds like a freedom-of-expression lawsuit to me.

Kite also wore, um, well, he used the technical term: "fake boobs." At least he said they were fake. Let's take his word for it.

"He looks pretty good," Melistas said, "except he should have shaved his armpits. That dress doesn't have any sleeves."

Kite might have shaved his armpits, had he been asked. He was a remarkably good sport about losing the bet. "I was going to do makeup, but I have to go to my other job after this," he said. "If you're going to do it, you might as well go all out."

Kite's other job is at Structure, a men's clothing store. He was working there during Game 6 when his cell phone kept going off with urgent messages from his Shell co-workers. Wings 1, Vancouver 0 . . . Wings 2, Vancouver 0. . . . "That's the first point I realized I was in trouble," he said.

He didn't realize how much trouble. When the Shell staff decided to order pizza for lunch, guess who was sent to pick it up? "And they keep sending me out to get parts," Kite said. "I normally don't do that."

Would Kite prefer to wear a dress or a Wings jersey? "Probably the dress," he said. "Everybody knows I'm a big Colorado fan. If I wore the jersey, I'd be betraying what I believe in."

Gritty, not pretty

BY MICHAEL ROSENBERG

Remember this feeling? It's been awhile, but surely you remember. Red Wings on the ice, you in your seat, game in the bag, panic medicine in the cabinet. This is what it was like for most of the season, when the Wings were the best team in hockey.

They were better again in Game 1 of their second-round playoff series against St. Louis. Not great, just the better team — the delightfully boring, calmly efficient team that gave you so many restful nights during the season.

"We got a 2-0 win, but I don't think that we necessarily played all that well," Steve Yzerman said. "And I don't think St. Louis played their best game. Kind of a strange game."

The Wings won thanks to three guys who weren't in Detroit during the last three playoff failures.

Brett Hull did what he was born to do — score when it seemed like nobody could. Hull unleashed a wrist shot that left a mark on goalie Brent Johnson, then scored on a rebound.

Rookie Pavel Datsyuk did what he will do for a long time — score a brilliant goal. He deked one Blue while another, Bryce Salvador, gave him a mugging. Datsyuk ended up with his first career playoff goal, and Salvador ended up

MANDI WRIGHT

Forward Sergei Fedorov and the Red Wings had enough to get past Chris Pronger and St. Louis in the second-round opener.

with Datsyuk's wallet.

And Dominik Hasek did what he was brought here to do. He made a couple of great saves and a bunch more he was supposed to make. And when the Wings had a 2-0 lead and the Blues started firing pucks at him, he looked like his old Dominating self.

Hasek admitted to being "a lit-

tle bit lucky. We scored two goals," he said, "and they hit the post three times."

The game ended with a series of fights — as you read this, they're still doling out penalties. But what mattered most is the Wings won. They picked up a ho-hum, no-news-is-good-news victory, and they hadn't done that in a while.

Hull-abaloo

Brett Hull, who had three goals in Game 6 against Vancouver and one against St. Louis in Game I, is, in his own words, "a guy with an opinion who's not afraid to say it, outspoken." His thoughts . . .

● On fitting in with the rest of the Red Wings: "I didn't come here thinking, 'Boy, I wonder if I'm going to fit in.' I'm here to play hockey."

● On whether the Wings initiated him: "After 1,000 games, you don't get initiated."

● On playing with Steve Yzerman: "He's been one of my favorite players, if not my favorite player, since I broke in the league."

● On practicing with Yzerman: "Stevie, one of the best players ever to play the game, might be the worst practice player in the history of the game."

● On whether the Blues are stronger now than when he played for them: "Of course not. Geez."

Luc's lucky day

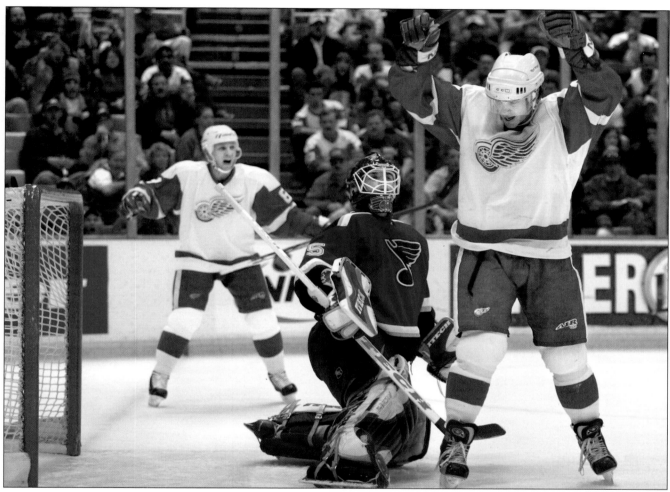

KIRTHMON F. DOZIER

A deflection by Red Wings forward Luc Robitaille, right, got the Game 2 winner past St. Louis' Brent Johnson.

BY NICHOLAS J. COTSONIKA

Luc Robitaille laughed as he described what turned out to be the winning goal in the Red Wings' 3-2 victory, which gave them a 2-0 lead in their second-round playoff series with St. Louis.

Fredrik Olausson fired a shot from the left point on the power play. Robitaille was in front. "I just was there," Robitaille said. "I've been there for two weeks." He laughed.

"It hit me," he said, and he laughed again.

The puck hit off the front right of Robitaille's sweater, past screened goaltender Brent Johnson and into the net. When the goal was announced as Robitaille's, the fans showed their love by showering him with the usual hearty "LUUUC!"

Robitaille, who assisted on Brett Hull's power-play goal earlier, hadn't gotten a point since scoring a goal in the playoff opener 17 days earlier. Six games and nothing. That wasn't good

for an offensive superstar with 675 goals, regular season and playoffs combined. But that's not the whole story, either.

Robitaille took 14 shifts in Game 2. Tomas Holmstrom, who took 12, was the only Wings skater with fewer. But Robitaille came to Detroit to win his first Stanley Cup, and he knew he was signing with a talent-laden team.

"I knew I'd have to give up something," Robitaille said. "I'm willing to do that. I just want to win."

Hats off to Blues

BY HELENE ST. JAMES

MANDI WRIGHT

Keith Tkachuk's trick brought a wave of hats from the St. Louis fans, and the torrent of goals eventually chased Red Wings goaltender Dominik Hasek.

ST. LOUIS — One hat sailed through the air, landing behind Dominik Hasek after Keith Tkachuk accomplished one of many firsts for the Blues in Game 3. Play resumed with the hat still on the ice as fans at the Savvis Center roared "HASEK! HASEK!" juiced because their team was only 18 minutes away from its first win of the series.

One fan among the 19,107 tossed another baseball cap. That started an avalanche that left hats of every color and yellow foam rods for cheering scattered on the ice, forcing a stoppage of play and an announcement that the Blues could get a penalty if the littering didn't stop. Fans obliged and settled for taunting Hasek.

"I was kind of begging for them to stop because I didn't want us to get a penalty," Tkachuk said.

His first playoff hat trick was one of many firsts by the Blues. They pounced first and grabbed a lead. And when it was erased, they regained it. They scored on their power plays (another first), going 2-for-5, and they shut down the Red Wings on theirs (Detroit was 0-for-6).

The result was a 6-1 victory that edged St. Louis back into the best-of-seven series, 2-1.

"We played the way we wanted to, and the results are there," Tkachuk said. His three goals "were nice, but the bottom line is we needed that win. We didn't want to go down by three games against a team like Detroit."

The Blues' final first of the series came directly from the pages of Detroit's playbook. With the Blues shorthanded, Pavol Demitra grabbed a pass from Chris Pronger and beat Hasek with a wrist shot. That prompted more ribbing of Hasek from the gleeful fans.

Scott Mellanby, who scored his third goal of the series, said, "A lot of things happened tonight that are good for our psyche."

Blues schmooze

Among the benefits of winning is the levity it breeds. The morning after their Game 3 victory, in one part of the Blues' dressing room, Doug Weight laughed when he realized there was a better way than saying "he's bi" to describe Pavol Demitra's knack for playing center and wing. In another area, Scott Mellanby, who had a goal and an assist, was downplaying his contributions.

"I'm just a slug that gets lucky enough to play with them," he said of his linemates, Demitra and Keith Tkachuk. "It's fun."

Wings fans might remember Mellanby's claim to fame as a Florida Panther. He slew a rat in the locker room, inspiring fans there to litter the ice with rubber rodents. So there will always be a place for him in the Hall of Fame — if they ever need help with pest control, that is.

Happy birthday

Jeff Finley and the Blues gave Brett Hull and the Red Wings their best shot in Game 4 — St. Louis scored two late goals to keep things interesting — but a lucky goal by captain Steve Yzerman put Detroit over the top.

JULIAN H. GONZALEZ

BY NICHOLAS J. COTSONIKA

ST. LOUIS — They had a rough start. They had a rough finish. But in between, the Red Wings scrounged enough to come out with a wild 4-3 victory and a 3-1 lead over the Blues, who lost their captain, Chris Pronger, for the rest of the playoffs. He suffered a torn anterior cruciate ligament in his right knee while trying to hit Steve Yzerman, who is playing on a bum right knee.

Yzerman ducked the hit from Pronger and later said: "Going down like that beats getting run over. It was really the only thing I could do. Unfortunately for Chris, when you're a tall guy like he is, you can take a pretty good fall on something like that."

The Blues had pressure early and three power plays. But they managed only one goal, by Scott Young during a two-man advantage, and Pronger went down soon afterward.

The Wings responded with goals by Brendan Shanahan, Jiri Fischer, Tomas Holmstrom and Yzerman. The eventual winner was pure luck, a gift for Yzerman on his 37th birthday.

During a Detroit power play early in the third period, goaltender Brent Johnson tried to clear the puck but failed. "It hit me in the stomach," Yzerman said, "and then it bounced off the defenseman's foot and in the net."

St. Louis' Scott Mellanby and Keith Tkachuk scored in the final 2:54. "I thought we played a real good game until the last three or four minutes," Yzerman said. "We kind of came apart a bit. We didn't play the last three minutes very well. Obviously we have to be much better in that type of situation."

Dominik Hasek made 33 saves — nine in the first 6½ minutes, 17 in the third period. "Dom came up huge for us," Chris Chelios said.

OCTOMETER

Observations on the Wings-Blues series (rated on a scale of one to four octopi):

A big happy birthday to the Captain, who turned 37 and gave the Blues a spanking.

Not that we believe in teams of destiny — or gloating over injuries — but doesn't the Pronger incident seem like one of those signs that things are going the Wings' way this year? Really, in a collision, who would have guessed Yzerman would be the last captain standing?

It's about character

MITCH ALBOM

Steve Yzerman is in his car, driving to practice between Games 4 and 5 of the St. Louis series. He doesn't really do much on the practice ice these days. For one thing, his bad knee can't take it. And, anyhow, at this point in the season, he and the other veterans don't exactly need work.

But he goes. He goes because "you're supposed to be there," he says. "If we have an 11 a.m. practice, it's not like I can show up at 11:15 and say, 'Hey, Scotty, how you doin'?' You can't take advantage of your status. Other guys won't say anything because they don't want to rock the boat, but they start wondering why they should be doing it if you're not. It creates dissension."

Funny. Another star athlete, the NBA's Allen Iverson — 10 years younger than Yzerman — recently complained that his coach, Larry Brown, was making too much of his skipping practices. "I'm the franchise player and we're talking about practice?" an angry Iverson said at a news conference. "Practice? . . . We're talking about practice?"

Well, actually they were talking about character, which almost oozes from Yzerman now. So much so that some observers tend to look at the Captain these days and all but gush, like the TV announcers who keep insisting that he is playing "on one leg."

Not quite. If you play on one leg, you fall. Yzerman is not a crippled, crawling-out-of-bed martyr. "I have a sore knee, and that's about it," he says. "It hasn't gotten better, but it hasn't gotten worse. I'm not playing on one leg or anything. That's just, ah, you know."

We know. It's a compliment.

You like to give Yzerman compliments, partly because he hates getting them so much. In Game 4 against the Blues, he played the kind of game that pushes teams to glory. Yes, he scored a goal (actually the goal scored off him), but the points mattered least. It was the effort. It was the resilience. It was the storm of collisions he weathered, many by design of the Blues, who wanted to nullify him.

Couldn't do it. They tried. Nobody harder than mammoth defenseman Chris Pronger, who attempted a slam that Yzerman evaded by ducking low like someone out of a Jackie Chan movie. Pronger flipped over him and landed on his right knee and out of

THE PLAYOFFS

Captain Steve Yzerman, sore knee and all — though nothing worse, despite the efforts of the Blues and Jamal Mayers — kept going to practices in which he could barely participate, and kept making the big plays to keep the Red Wings on track.

the playoffs with a torn ACL.

"That was a fluky thing," Yzerman says from his car. "You don't want to see anyone get hurt."

Yzerman knows the other side. In another year, he might have been the one hobbling off. It has happened. Too many times. But in these playoffs, he's still standing. Neither he nor his teammates have suffered any good-bye blows.

So it was a good night for Yzerman — and to boot, it was his 37th birthday. He flew back with the team, got in his car and drove home. If he were proud of himself, it could be expected. After all, playing among kids 10 and 15 years younger, he was perhaps the best player out there.

So how did he celebrate?

"Actually," he says, approaching downtown Detroit, "the only thought I gave to my birthday was that when I came into the league, the Wings had just acquired Brad Park. And I had always looked up to Brad Park. But he was 37 at the time. I thought, 'Wow. He's 37. He's got a wife and family. He's an old guy.' And now that's me."

He laughs, and through the cell phone you hear the wind from outside. You realize this is slowly coming to an end, this era of veterans like Yzerman, sticking in one city their whole careers, going to practice on sunny days without complaint. He is, so far, having the playoffs of his dreams, leading the Red Wings in goals, points, game-winners — and respect.

Bye-Bye, Blues

MANDI WRIGHT

Red Wings forward Brett Hull congratulated goalie Dominik Hasek, left, on his Game 5 shutout, Hasek's third of the playoffs.

BY NICHOLAS J. COTSONIKA

The Red Wings chased away the Blues. They won the game, 4-0. They won the series, 4-1. And they advanced to the Western Conference finals for the first time since 1998, when they won their second straight Stanley Cup.

Brendan Shanahan had two goals, including an empty-netter, and two assists. Jiri Fischer had a goal and an assist. Tomas Holmstrom also scored. Chris Chelios also had two assists. The shutout was goaltender Dominik Hasek's third of the playoffs.

Hasek said St. Louis "wasn't the same team" without captain Chris Pronger, who suffered a torn anterior cruciate ligament in his right knee in Game 4. Hasek said the Blues didn't play as hard as they had before.

After almost blowing three-goal third-period leads in Games 2 and 4, the Wings had no problem with a two-goal lead in this one. They were more aggressive.

"You just can't afford to sit back and not generate any offense," Steve Yzerman said.

Following the game, the Wings were able to take a bit of a rest — especially Yzerman, who had been playing with a sore right knee, and Igor Larionov, who had a leg injury.

"I think it will help those guys," Scotty Bowman said. "Obviously, we wanted to win very badly so we wouldn't have to go back to St. Louis."

Go Avs!

Kris Draper a Colorado fan? He was when the Wings eliminated St. Louis and San Jose held a 3-2 series lead over the Avalanche in the other Western Conference semifinal. Draper was among those cheering for Colorado to beat the Sharks and prolong the series.

"Believe it or not, that's what we want to see," Draper said with a grin. "We've been watching some of their games, and they've been going at it pretty good. So we're cheering for Colorado to win Game 6 and make it a seven-game series."

Draper got his wish when Colorado forced Game 7 and the Wings received a week off before resuming play against the Avs.

MANDI WRIGHT

St. Louis was the Red Wings' gateway to the Western Conference finals, and the Burgesses — dad John, taking picture, and kids Jennifer and Jeff — made the trip from Bangor, Michigan, for Game 4.

Old friends

The Red Wings-Avalanche rivalry heated up in 1996, when Colorado beat the Wings in the conference finals and Claude Lemieux smashed Kris Draper's face into the boards. This would be their fifth playoff meeting in seven seasons. The Avs had won three of the previous four. What happened in those series:

1996: The Wings set a record for regular-season victories with 62, but the Avs beat them in six games in the Western Conference finals. Colorado won the first two games at Joe Louis Arena — in overtime in Game 1, in a Patrick Roy shutout in Game 2. The Wings came back to flail Roy with six goals in Game 3 and five in Game 5, but they lost the finale, 4-1, at Denver. That's when Lemieux rearranged Draper's face by pushing him from behind. The Avs swept Florida in the Stanley Cup finals.

TOM PIDGEON/ASSOCIATED PRESS

1997: Three weeks before the playoffs, the Wings retaliated for the Draper hit in a March 26 bloodbath at Joe Louis Arena. Darren McCarty went after Lemieux in the first period, and the teams brawled. Even the goalies — Roy, above, and Mike Vernon — fought. That set up a playoff rematch in the conference finals, which the Wings won in six games. They took a 3-1 series lead with a 6-0 victory in Detroit, then lost, 6-0, at Colorado. But when the Wings returned home, they clinched the series with a 3-1 victory. They went on to sweep Philadelphia for their first Stanley Cup in 42 years.

1999: The Wings appeared in command after winning the first two games at Colorado in the second round, but they proceeded to lose four straight in a stunning reversal. Goalie Bill Ranford, who shut out the Avs in Game 2, took 5-3 and 6-2 losses in Detroit. Roy got a shutout in Game 5, then beat the Wings, 5-2, in Game 6 at Joe Louis Arena.

2000: For the second straight year, the teams met in the second round, and the Avs won again, this time in five games. The killer for the Wings came in Game 4, when they lost in overtime, 3-2, at Joe Louis Arena. That gave the Avs a 3-1 series lead. Colorado finished the series at home with a 4-2 victory.

McCarty party

BY HELENE ST. JAMES

H is first goal was cheered. His second was greeted by wild applause and an octopus. His third resulted in the ice at Joe Louis Arena being littered with hats and octopi, real and man-made, as 20,058 partisans erupted in a party.

The production was as much a surprise to the Colorado Avalanche as to the delighted scorer. After five goals in 62 regular-season games, Darren McCarty pulled off a natural hat trick in less than 15 minutes in the third period, giving Detroit a 5-3 victory and 1-0 lead in the Western Conference finals.

"You've all read the Bible and heard of the Apocalypse?" McCarty said, smiling. "It's my first hat trick. It's huge. But the bottom line is, you take the win first. This is an unbelievable team we're playing. It's one game, and it's nice to have won it, but we know from history we have to keep playing hard."

McCarty scored his first play-off goal of the season at 1:18 of the third period when Patrick Roy misjudged the shot. He scored again at 12:44 on a slap shot from the right circle that flew past Roy's left shoulder, and once more when he fired in Kirk Maltby's rebound with 4:05 left.

"It's a wonderful effort from a guy that gives his all every game," Scotty Bowman said. "They were all great goals against one of the greatest goaltenders who ever played the game. There wasn't

Forward Darren McCarty scored his first goal and broke a third-period tie at 2 with Colorado . . .

. . . then beat Colorado goaltender Patrick Roy to put them up, 4-2, just more than 11 minutes later . . .

PHOTOS BY JULIAN H. GONZALEZ

. . . and finally beat Roy a third time with 4:05 left. "It's a wonderful effort from a guy that gives his all every game," Scotty Bowman said. "They were all great goals against one of the greatest goaltenders who ever played the game."

The music man

BY DAVID LYMAN

He is the Wings' seventh man. He has no stick, no skates, no pads.

Just eight tape decks, a box full of mini-discs and a musical sense as attuned to the fans' moods as Dominik Hasek is attuned to Colorado's big shooters.

Tim Campbell — T, as he's known professionally — grabs a mini-disc off the top of his console, hurriedly spins a couple of knobs and, suddenly, the arena is filled with the furious sound of "The Launch," a hard-driving piece of techno by DJ Jean.

The video screen above center ice screams "NOISE," and the crowd erupts. They're on their feet, bellowing so loudly they threaten to send the Red Wings' Noise-o-meter ricocheting to the top of the scale.

And just as immediately, the game kicks into high gear, the thumping and pounding every bit as intense as the sounds blaring out of the public address system.

"We're really not very aware of the music when we're on the ice," Nicklas Lidstrom said. "But the music gets the crowd going. And when the crowd is loud, it really helps us. It's like an extra push,

PAUL GONZALEZ VIDELA

"It doesn't get any better than this, does it?" DJ Tim Campbell said of rocking Joe Louis. "It's like one big party."

extra energy."

Just 1:18 into the third period of Game 1 against Colorado, Darren McCarty scores the first of what will be three goals. The mood in the arena is jubilant. The goal is the reason, of course. But Campbell enhances it with a quick-cutting montage of hard-driving rock — a musical parallel to McCarty's pounding, playing style.

Then, for good measure, he tosses in a snippet of "Mack the Knife."

McCarty scores again. Campbell pulls up "Twilight Zone," by 2 Unlimited. It's wonderfully frantic.

Miraculously, the usually low-scoring McCarty scores a third time. Now it's time for "1, 2, 3," by Len Barry.

The crowd sings along.

THE PLAYLIST

Tim Campbell, official disc jockey for Red Wings home games, calls them "situational selections" — songs he pulls from the 1,400 tunes he has on hand to add dramatic flair to a specific situation on the ice. They include:

- "The Night Chicago Died," by Paper Lace. When the Wings beat the Blackhawks, of course.
- "I Guess That's Why They Call It the Blues," by Elton John. When the Wings beat the Blues, as they did in Round 2.
- "Just the Two of Us," by Will Smith. Played when opposing players are sent to the penalty box.
- "Piano Man," by Billy Joel. At Saturday night games, Campbell will often set his timer for 9 p.m. Why? The lyrics: "It's nine o'clock on a Saturday. . . ."
- "Waltz of the Flowers," from Tchaikovsky's "Nutcracker." Played when the opposing team returns to the ice between periods.
- "Signs," by the Five Man Electrical Band. Because of the lyrics — "Long-haired freaky people need not apply" — it's often used to tweak scraggly haired players like Mike Ricci of San Jose or the Blues' Tyson Nash.
- "Hold Me, Thrill Me, Kiss Me," by Mel Carter. Played when the opposing team is penalized for holding.

"It doesn't get any better than this, does it?" Campbell says. "It's like one big party."

J. KYLE KEENER

Avalanche fan Carlo DeRose of Windsor, left, suffered the mocks of Red Wings fans during Game 1.

anything lucky about any of them."

The Wings also got goals from Tomas Holmstrom and Brett Hull, and 24 saves from Dominik Hasek.

Roy said, "I played good," after finishing with 25 saves while being subjected to "Pa-trick!" taunts every time he allowed a goal and numerous "Hasek's better!" chants from the fans. Joe Sakic scored on one of his game-high five shots, and Colorado also got goals from Milan Hejduk and Alex Tanguay.

Thanks, Dad

Darren McCarty's son, Griffin, celebrated his sixth birthday two days after Dad scored the hat trick. McCarty gave him the game puck and let him sort through the hats that had been collected to see if he wanted any.

"He put a lot of pressure on me — he wanted a goal," McCarty said with a grin. Teammates high-fived Griffin after the game and Chris Chelios asked, "What did your daddy eat for breakfast?"

Before the game, Luc Robitaille picked out a stick for McCarty to use, and McCarty credited video coordinator and former teammate Joe Kocur for putting "a voodoo hex" on it.

Father knows best

BY MICHAEL ROSENBERG

Father Pat Casey began seeing signs in the middle of mass. Nobody else saw them. They bore messages he felt he needed to share with his parishioners. Urgent messages.

And so, in the middle of mass, he intoned: "Red Wings 3, Avalanche 2."

And then, "Red Wings 4, Avalanche 2."

And then the Red Wings won Game 1.

And the crowd was pleased.

And Father Casey, wearing a winged wheel on his vestment, was pleased as well.

Casey, a die-hard Wings fan, arranged for a neighbor to hold up signs in the back of his church, St. Dominic's. (No, not Hasek.) He frequently mentioned the Wings when addressing his congregation.

Of course, this mixture of church and sports did not go over well with some people.

"I have had complaints from my parishioners who are Detroit Piston fans," said Father Casey, whose parish is at Trumbull and Warren in Detroit. "They said I didn't do enough to promote the Pistons."

Casey, who might be the wittiest priest in southeast Michigan, didn't want anybody to get the wrong idea. He did not preach for the Red Wings. He did not say God is a Wings fan.

"I have never prayed for the

PHOTOS BY J. KYLE KEENER

**Above: A Red Wings banner shares wall space with a crucifix at St. Dominic's in Detroit.
Left: Father Pat Casey wears a winged-wheel vestment during mass.**

God that Darren McCarty got a hat trick," Father Casey cracked.

The priest had no plans to get a Lions or Tigers vestment.

"Hockey is the only one," Casey said. "There is no reason to be a football fan in Detroit. There is very little reason to be a baseball fan in Detroit. And I never could seem to get into basketball."

Father Casey said his favorite Wing is probably Chris Chelios. He admitted that when you need an urgent answer to a hockey trivia question, he is not your man. He's simply a priest who happens to be a Wings fan.

And he made no apologies for mentioning the Wings when he spoke to his parish.

"I think there is a natural link between praising God and athletes' pushing their bodies to limits," he said. "Sports celebrate accomplishment. People reach beyond themselves through athletics. It's all very akin to our relationship to God. Sports is a wonderful way to give glory to God. I don't see anything wrong with it at all."

What would he think if a priest in Denver did the same thing with the Avs that he does with the Wings? Would he understand?

"I'm not sure God would understand," he said, "but I would understand."

Red Wings to win," he said.

He had come close. For example: "May God continue to inspire the Red Wings as they inspire our city to great things."

Casey, who grew up in Waterford, said he uses the Wings as a metaphor.

"For Pentecost Sunday, I likened the gifts of the Holy Spirit to the myriad of gifts that Red Wings players have," he said. "My parishioners are used to my goofy analogies. I'm not preaching for the Red Wings. I just try to use them so people understand what I'm talking about.

"I don't mind at all being the center of attention, but more importantly I'm trying to draw attention to the ministry," he said.

Any other motives?

"I'm always looking for people to give me free tickets to the games," he said. "I'm just a mooch."

So this wasn't about divine intervention for Mike Ilitch's team?

"Well, it must be the work of

Drury night

BY MICHAEL ROSENBERG

KIRTHMON F. DOZIER

Colorado's Chris Drury was back to his old moves in Game 2 as he scored the winning goal — his fourth career winning playoff goal against the Red Wings.

ENGLEWOOD, Colo. — When Chris Drury beat Dominik Hasek with the winning goal in Game 2, he reacted as though he had not done anything impressive.

You didn't think he'd be surprised, did you?

Drury must be used to it. He's only 25, but he has scored 10 winning playoff goals — four against the Red Wings. He has scored three overtime playoff goals and has scored winning goals in Game 7 against the Los Angeles Kings in each of the past two years.

The Game 2 winner was classic Drury. He took a pass from Steven Reinprecht and found nobody between himself and Hasek. He seemed like he was in great position. But not great enough for his tastes. "Some guys — most guys probably — would have shot that right away," Reinprecht said. "But he faked the shot, moved a little bit to his right and gave himself a good net to shoot at."

Drury's goal at 2:17 is a prime example of why the Avs are so much tougher than most playoff teams. They rarely lose their poise. But neither did the Red Wings.

After rallying from one-goal deficits in the first two periods of their 5-3 Game 1 victory, the Wings rallied from a one-goal deficit each period in Game 2. Alex Tanguay scored on a power play at 2:59 of the first; Boyd Devereaux responded at 9:37. Peter Forsberg scored at 7:33 of the second; Kirk Maltby responded

shorthanded at 14:08. Greg de Vries scored at 5:26 of the third; Nicklas Lidstrom responded on a power play at 13:25.

But goaltender Patrick Roy improved to 9-0 since 1996 after allowing five or more goals the previous playoff game — the Avs improved to 10-0 — and the Wings lost for the second time in 11 games.

JULIAN H. GONZALEZ

The last time the Wings and Avs met in the playoffs, in 2000, Drury scored the biggest goal of the series in overtime of Game 4 at Joe Louis Arena. It gave Colorado a 3-1 series lead, and the Avs wrapped things up in Game 5 in Denver. "Chris Drury is one of the best money players we can have on our team," coach Bob Hartley said. "Whenever we need a big goal, Chris is always there for us."

The Avs' Adam Foote took this opportunity to reintroduce himself in front of the net to Darren McCarty during overtime.

Bad to the bone

BY STEVE SCHRADER

The Red Wings' pregame show at home was a work in progress — the longer they were in the playoffs, the bigger it got.

There was a light show, octopi hanging from the rafters, Hockeytown flagbearers — and Alto Reed, of Bob Seger's Silver Bullet Band, who did a saxophone solo on skates.

"It's an incredible feeling to skate around that arena, picking up on the energy of the fans, the team, to be the guy that pumps it up and gets it going," Reed said.

Reed was added in the second round when team president Denise Ilitch decided it was time to turn it up a notch — like when Karen Newman used to bungee-jump before singing the national anthem.

"I'm a huge, huge rock 'n' roll hockey fan," Reed said. "I grew up in Detroit, with 'Hockey Night in Canada.' . . . For me, hockey is bad to the bone, an awesome sport."

Wearing a "Reed 93" home jersey — from the first time he played "The Star-Spangled Banner" at the Joe, for a New Year's Eve game in 1993 — he skated around the rink, playing a three-part medley: "a sax wail to the gods of the Stanley Cup," the opening line from Seger's "Turn the Page" and then Def Leppard's "Back in Your Face."

And he really was playing — "none of that pantomime stuff" —

KIRTHMON F. DOZIER

Playing a saxophone solo on skates at Joe Louis Arena, Alto Reed had to worry about catching an edge as well as hitting his notes.

even though he said it wasn't as easy as it might've looked. "No matter how many times you do it, every time is like the first time," Reed said of the anthem. "That's always lingering, looming, like 'Oh, man, do it right.' And this is compounded by 'OK, man, don't catch an edge.' "

Reed said he really got his choreography down for Game 1 against Colorado, but . . .

"As I was coming off the ice . . . I think it was (Darius) Kasparaitis that came up behind me and gave me a little tap with the stick on the rear, like 'OK, pal, nice job, get the hell out of here.' "

Bad form

Colorado coach Bob Hartley sat on the bench and watched the Red Wings practice before Game 2. "I try to stay up-to-date with what's going on out there," Hartley said. "I'm looking for little details that could be useful to us in the future games."

That's considered bad form, even if there is no rule against it. If a coach wants to watch the opposition practice, he usually does it in the stands. But Scotty Bowman said he didn't mind. Hartley was on the Avalanche bench, after all. Anyway, "He's a friendly guy," Bowman said of Hartley. "He's not uptight."

Asked if Bowman said anything to him while he was sitting there, Hartley said, "Oh, he just said, 'Hi.' Like, we're close friends." Asked if Bowman offered him coffee and doughnuts, Hartley joked, "Maybe some fried octopus."

JULIAN H. GONZALEZ

Colorado coach Bob Hartley had a friendly smile for his Detroit counterpart as he watched the Red Wings practice.

THE PLAYOFFS

How Swede it is

Tired of having his vision blocked by the pestering presence of Tomas Holmstrom, Colorado goalie Patrick Roy retaliated with a left jab.

JULIAN H. GONZALEZ

BY MITCH ALBOM AND NICHOLAS J. COTSONIKA

DENVER — A year earlier at about this time, Fredrik Olausson had been in a hospital bed in Bern, Switzerland, with a ruptured spleen. The idea of scoring an overtime goal in the Western Conference finals was as likely as his getting up and doing the rumba.

But time passed and things changed, and here he was in overtime, taking a pass from Steve Yzerman and lining up a big slap shot that somehow did what all the other great Detroit shots could not do on this night — get past Colorado's Patrick Roy.

"Did you even watch the playoffs last year?" someone asked Olausson in the upbeat Red Wings locker room after his goal won Game 3 and gave the Wings a precious 2-1 series lead.

"Did I watch the playoffs?" he said, laughing. "No. I couldn't. They didn't have satellite TV in the hospital."

Freddie Olausson? He scored the winner? That's right. He did. The guy who doesn't get mentioned when people talk about Detroit's off-season acquisitions. They say Hull. They say Robitaille. They say Hasek.

And they say, "Oh, yeah, there's another free agent, a Swede, right?"

A Swede indeed. Olausson got a phone call in the spring of 2001 from the Red Wings. He had been out of the NHL. He'd been playing in Switzerland. He wasn't even sure he'd go back to North America.

But when he heard Detroit, he looked at his wife "and she just nodded," he said. "She said, 'You can't pass up this opportunity.' "

Back he came. Over the water. Into the Midwest. And in Game 3,

Priceless, eh?

The MasterCard people probably didn't have this type of stuff in mind when they adopted the "priceless" ad campaign, but the format just seems to work perfectly for sports insults. The phony ad here is one of those anonymous Internet jokes that arrived in our Freep e-mail. No offense to Mrs. Roy, but not bad, eh?

Detroit Red Wings

Two tickets to the Pepsi Center in Denver: $250

One hot dog to choke on because Greg DeVries throws the puck in his own net : $3.00

12 beers to drown your sorrows: $45

The look on your face as your husband lets in the overtime goal to lose game 3........ PRICELESS!!!

GO WINGS!!!

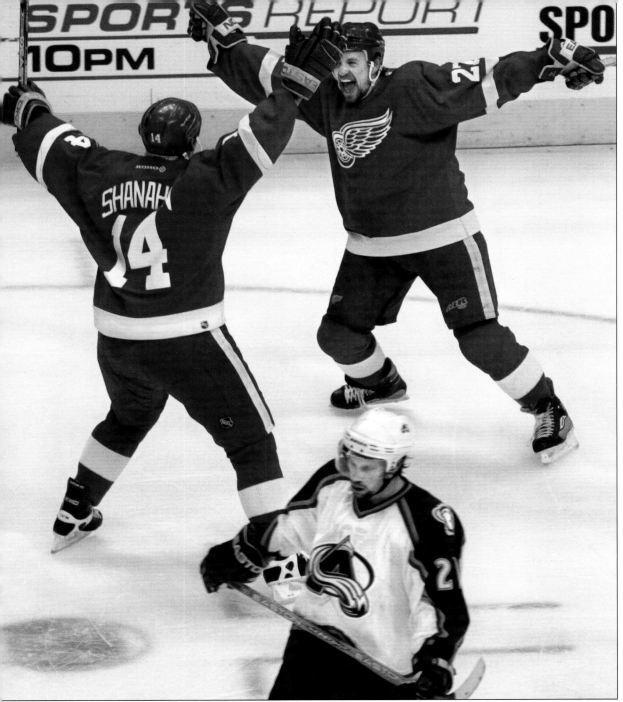

A joyous gravitation drew Brendan Shanahan and Fredrik Olausson together after Olausson's overtime goal. Colorado's Peter Forsberg orbited away dejectedly.

KIRTHMON F. DOZIER

he applied that "don't miss the opportunity" theory to the max. His goal, nearly 13 minutes into overtime, was his first playoff goal in 10 years.

"We were skating really hard tonight, offensively and defensively as well," said Luc Robitaille, who broke his own goal-less streak with a ricochet off his skate in the third period that would have made a pinball envious. The shot originat-

ed off Sergei Fedorov's stick, then hit Roy, hit another Av, hit another Av, hit Robitaille's skate and went in.

"I'll take it," Robitaille said.

The Wings controlled the play almost all night. They had a 34-16 shots advantage through regulation. But they had to go to OT because Rob Blake had given the Avs a 1-0 lead in the first period with a power-play deflection.

In the end, the Wings outshot the Avs, 42-21, and while Scotty Bowman said his Wings skated "a lot better," coach Bob Hartley said his Avs "didn't skate."

"I think it's pretty clear that we had no business being in it," Hartley said. Roy "gave us every chance possible to go home with a victory that we didn't deserve. The Red Wings outplayed us and outworked us, plain and simple."

THE PLAYOFFS

Czechmate

JULIAN H. GONZALEZ

Defenseman Jiri Fischer, here receiving congratulations from teammate Sergei Fedorov, learned quickly to forget poor games — as well as good ones.

DREW SHARP

DENVER — Not only were Jiri Fischer's teammates counting on him, but his country was as well.

Dominik Hasek was already a national icon in the Czech Republic. He was honored with a parade in 1998 after leading his country to the Olympic gold medal. Fischer remembered well how business stopped and schools closed around his hometown of Prague as everyone watched the televised games from Nagano, Japan.

When Hasek made his first appearance in the Stanley Cup finals in 1999, Czechs everywhere watched the live broadcasts.

So what if they began at 3 a.m. local time?

"The Olympics were much bigger because it brought the whole country together," said Fischer. "But Dominik looking for his first Stanley Cup is probably the next biggest because everyone looks up to Dominik so much. He's a hero in our country. He's represented us so well. It's been a great honor for me to play with him because I learn so much watching how he prepares himself mentally for each game."

One attribute Fischer learned was the ability to quickly forget poor games, as well as the good ones. Finding perspective was

THE PLAYOFFS

important after Fischer took three penalties and was a minus-3 in Colorado's 4-3 overtime victory in Game 2. The disappointment came and went. Fischer put it out of his mind and quickly rebounded with his best playoff effort in the Wings' 2-1 overtime win in Game 3.

Fischer finally did what his teammates couldn't — knock Peter Forsberg off stride. He compiled a team-high 12 hits, blocked four shots and raised his playoff plus/minus rating to plus-3. Not a bad recovery, considering he was minus-4 after the two opening losses to Vancouver in the first round.

Hasek "made a point to tell me afterward," Fischer said, "that how someone responds to a mistake is sometimes more important than making the mistake itself. You want to learn from it and not do it again."

Game 3 "was a big step forward in Jiri's maturation," associate coach Dave Lewis said. "Emotions are inevitable in the playoffs, especially at this juncture. But the key is playing within those emotions, and I thought Jiri did a great job of maintaining that discipline. He played his kind of game, physical, blocking shots and controlling the puck without overextending himself and potentially making mistakes."

Fischer — 6-feet-5, 210 pounds — played 26 minutes, 42 seconds in Game 3, a personal playoff high.

"Part of my job of being paired with Jiri is to help him through the rough times," said Chris Chelios, nearly 20 years Fischer's senior. "But I didn't have to say much to him after Game 2. He already knew. His recognition of what he needs to do is better than last year. And you can only develop that through playing and learning."

The king of Sweden

MANDI WRIGHT

After taking the regular season off because of injury, Peter Forsberg was a playoff force to be reckoned with by the Red Wings.

BY MICHAEL ROSENBERG

DENVER — Lars Moberg of Sveriges Television in Sweden attended Game 3, working on a story about Sweden's favorite hockey player. And it wasn't Nicklas Lidstrom. Moberg was at the game because of Peter Forsberg.

Like Lidstrom, Forsberg is one of the best players in the world. But while Lidstrom is popular in Sweden, Forsberg is Michael Jordan-popular.

"Lidstrom is big, too, but I would say nobody is as big as Forsberg," Moberg said. "I think the Swedish nation was in shock mode on the 15th of September 2001, when he announced he wouldn't play (during the regular season). And the media overdid that so it looked like he would be out of the game forever — he was retiring, he was getting out of it. Peter never intended that, I'm sure."

Swedes (and many others) think of Forsberg as the best player in the world. But he's not just a popular athlete — he's a national hero.

"Everybody remembers the goal he scored against Canada to decide the Olympic tournament in Lillehammer in 1994," Moberg said.

In fact, Swedes are reminded of it when they open their mail — the Forsberg goal has been immortalized on a postage stamp.

Forsberg — a.k.a. Foppa, a.k.a. The Magic Boy — is a walking, skating fairy tale. His father was one of Sweden's most celebrated coaches. To top it off, there was this gem from the Avalanche media guide: "His grandfather, Henneng Sandsquist, is a legend in Norra, Sweden, for performing astounding feats of strength."

Would Moberg do a story on Lidstrom while in Denver?

"Not now," he said. "Our story now is on Forsberg. But I might even talk to Lidstrom about Forsberg, actually."

Avs pull even

JULIAN H. GONZALEZ

Sprawl as he might, Dominik Hasek couldn't stop Peter Forsberg's go-ahead goal, and Jiri Fischer could only watch.

BY NICHOLAS J. COTSONIKA AND DREW SHARP

DENVER — Colorado captain Joe Sakic took a pass, sped into the Detroit zone and fired a shot past the right pad of Dominik Hasek 45 seconds into the third period. It was the turning point of Game 4, a 3-2 Avalanche victory that tied the Western Conference finals at 2.

The score was tied at 1 when Sakic tallied, but the Red Wings had been dominating. After two periods, the Wings led in shots, 25-12. They looked as good as they did in Game 3.

"Once again, we saw why the Detroit Red Wings were by far the best team in the regular season," Colorado coach Bob Hartley said. "They were flying. They were on the puck."

"We expected them to come out with their best game of the series, and that's exactly what happened," Steve Yzerman said. "It's disappointing, but it shouldn't surprise anyone that after four games, we're tied with each of us getting one win in the other guy's building."

"I don't want to think about what might have happened had we lost," Sakic said. "Because we didn't."

After coming close several times, the Avs took a 3-1 lead — their first two-goal lead of the series — with 3:17 left. Peter Forsberg flew down the right wing and flipped the puck to Chris Drury, who was streaking down the middle of the ice and redirected the puck past Hasek's left shoulder.

The Wings pulled Hasek with 2:52 left and went at goaltender Patrick Roy with everything they had. But they failed to score until three seconds remained, when Brett Hull beat Roy from in close.

"We pressed right to the end," Scotty Bowman said. "I was very proud of our team. You look at how they play. ... We played well but didn't win. I know that's not good enough, but it's always worse if you lose and play poorly. Then you have to change everything around. We don't have to change a lot."

Close shave

When Darren McCarty turned 30 on April 1, 2002, Kris Draper gave him a birthday cake — right in the face. McCarty promised he would have his revenge when Draper turned 31 on May 24 — the day before Game 4 in Denver. Draper said he would "just have to be ready."

As Draper was stretching at the end of practice, he sensed trouble — a towel full of shaving cream headed his way. ("We couldn't find a cake or a pie," McCarty said.) Draper took evasive action, and afterward, as he sat in the dressing room, he had a huge smile. "I foiled his plans," Draper said. "I'm a little smarter than him."

Kris Draper

McCarty chipped in, "He knows — he knows that payback's coming. Get 'em when they least expect it. I still owe him. I'll get him back."

THE PLAYOFFS

Missed opportunity

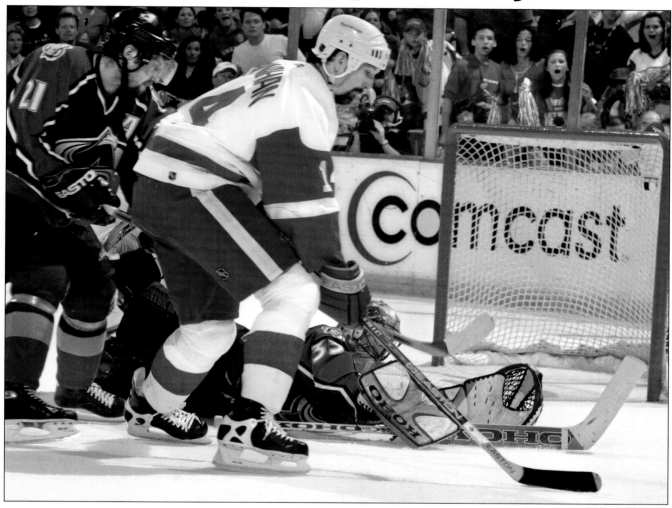

JULIAN H. GONZALEZ

Brendan Shanahan had a wide open net to shoot at with 1:40 left in regulation, but the toe of Peter Forsberg's stick tipped the puck, which hit the right post. "I'll have a nightmare about that one tonight," Shanahan said.

BY NICHOLAS J. COTSONIKA

In stunned silence, hundreds of fans stayed in their seats as the Avalanche celebrated at Joe Louis Arena. After coming within inches of victory, the Red Wings made a crucial mistake, and Peter Forsberg capitalized with a controversial goal 6:24 into overtime.

The Wings lost, 2-1, and trailed the Western finals, 3-2.

"It was an angry group in the dressing room after the game ob-

viously," Brendan Shanahan said. "But we haven't turned on each other. We're not quitting. We're staying positive, and tomorrow we're going to shake this one off and start thinking about the next game."

Shanahan had perhaps the most to shake off. With 1:40 left in regulation, he skated through the slot, stickhandled past defenseman Rob Blake and drew goaltender Patrick Roy out toward the right circle. He was on a sharp

angle but had an open net.

He hit the right post.

On the bench afterward, he looked skyward. "I'll have a nightmare about that one tonight," said Shanahan, who hadn't scored in the series. "I was shocked it didn't go in because I saw the empty net. I waited and waited till everyone went down. I didn't know how it didn't go in. I was about to turn and put my arms up in the air.

"I saw the replay after the period, and one of the backcheckers"

THE PLAYOFFS

— it turned out to be Forsberg — "just got the toe of his blade on the puck as I was shooting it. Just changed the direction a little bit, and it caught the post instead of the net.

"Those ones really hurt."

After pressuring the Avs early in overtime — taking the first four shots — the Wings got caught on a line change. "Our left winger was coming off, and they threw it quickly up to their right winger," Steve Yzerman said.

The result was a 4-on-2. Brian Willsie, in his second career play-off game, tried to pass to Chris Drury. Jiri Fischer challenged Drury, and the puck went between Drury's legs — right to Forsberg.

"He was alone," Yzerman said.

Forsberg scored on the Avs' first OT shot, but Scotty Bowman thought the play was offside. Bowman said linesman Brian Murphy wasn't on the line. But Bowman added, "You can't blame Murphy. . . . It was a quick play — it's a tough call. I'm not going to cry over a call like that. That's the breaks in the game, and that's it."

None of the Wings used the call as an excuse. As Yzerman said, "It was pretty close. Too late now."

The Avs took a 1-0 lead in the first thanks to Steven Reinprecht. The Wings came back from a one-goal deficit for the eighth time this

GABRIEL B. TAIT

Colorado's Darius Kasparaitis had plenty to cheer about after Peter Forsberg's overtime goal gave the Avs a 2-1 victory and a 3-2 series lead.

series, thanks to Yzerman.

"We started poorly in the game," Yzerman said. "But we really stuck with it and climbed back into the game to a point where we had our chances to win

it. It's a tough loss, but we fully expected to be in a difficult series. I would've hoped to be up, 3-2, but being down, 3-2, I certainly don't feel like we're done or anything like that."

Words of wisdom

After Game 5, some in the Wings family were distraught. Some were not.

BRENDAN SHANAHAN: "After the game . . . our locker room was as angry as I've seen it all year. We were angry because we felt we deserved to win. We were angry because we had them back on their heels. We were angry because we had all kinds of chances in their end — and then they get one rush, one lucky pass that isn't even meant for the guy, one great chance, and they score.

"And now we have to forget about it. . . . You know, our team has played absolutely good hockey this series. We haven't had one game where we've been flat. We've come back constantly from one-goal deficits. We just have to think about winning one game.

"And once we take care of Game 6, then we'll take care of Game 7."

BUDD LYNCH, 84, the Joe Louis Arena public-address announcer and former broadcaster, who has lived through seven decades of tight moments involving the Red Wings: "Colorado are the defending champs. They are good. But every game has involved luck. Roy is not an invincible man. He can be beaten."

J. KYLE KEENER

Budd Lynch has been the voice of the Red Wings on radio and on the Joe Louis Arena public address system.

InDomitable

KIRTHMON F. DOZIER

Dominik Hasek stopped all 24 Colorado shots, including at least one with his face mask, in Game 6. "We have no doubts about our goaltender," Steve Yzerman said. "None."

BY MITCH ALBOM

DENVER — From the opening minutes to the closing horn, the message was as clear as a telegram:

Not done. Stop. Not losing. Stop. The Red Wings are not hitting the golf course. Stop. The Avalanche is not dancing into the Stanley Cup finals. Stop. There would be a Game 7 because one team was not ready to give up on its destiny, and one man was more than ready to face his own. Stop.

"When this team loses, people say we're old. And when we win, they say we're experienced," said a laughing Darren McCarty, who scored the Wings' second goal in Detroit's 2-0 Game 6 thriller that pushed the Western Conference finals to a finale at Joe Louis Arena. "But the thing is, we are experienced. We've been in these situations before. You have to think of it as just one hockey game.

"And then you have to go and win it."

That they did, for a myriad of reasons, but one stands a mask above the rest: On a night when the Red Wings needed 37-year-old

Colorado goalie Patrick Roy thought he had the puck in his glove, but it had fallen out and was sliding toward the net when Brendan Shanahan nudged it in for the Wings' first goal in Game 6.

Dominik Hasek to deliver $8 million worth of goaltending, he did.

"We have no doubts about our goaltender," Steve Yzerman said. "None."

Hasek was glue and rock and concrete and granite. He had never won a Stanley Cup, but there is a time for history, and this was a time to make some of your own. So here was Hasek, pitching his first shutout of the Western Conference finals, turning away all 24 shots, stopping the deadly Joe Sakic at point-blank range, stopping him again by blocking a flip shot, stopping him again while on his stomach.

Here was Hasek smothering a wraparound attempt by Chris Drury. Here was Hasek falling on another Drury shot not two feet from his body. He stopped the Avs on four power plays. He stopped the Avs when they pulled their goalie. He stopped them from all angles. From all distances.

In short, Hasek was superhuman. Patrick Roy was something less.

In the first period, after Steve Yzerman fired a close-range shot, Roy stopped it and was so sure he had it in his glove, he rose up in triumph.

Then, like a Little Leaguer who had his eyes closed on the pop-up, he opened his glove and — oops — there was nothing there. The puck was sliding behind him, heading for the net.

Brendan Shanahan spotted it, finished it off, and the Wings had two things they have not had in this series. The first goal. And a crucial Roy mistake.

"You said if you got another great chance, you wouldn't miss this time," a TV reporter told Shanahan in the locker room afterward.

"Well, it's pretty hard to miss from there," Shanahan said. "I'd have had to hang up my skates if I missed that one."

And after that, the Wings were untouchable. For one 20-minute stretch, they outshot the Avalanche, 18-1. Their defense was tight. Their penalty-killing was notable. Sergei Fedorov did an excellent job of thankless puck pursuit. Tomas Holmstrom took more front-of-the-net punishment than any man should have to endure.

It was little things. It was big things. It was as efficient and professional a performance as you could hope for from a hockey team.

Stick it to 'em

JULIAN H. GONZALEZ

Colorado coach Bob Hartley thought Dominik Hasek's stick blade might be a silly millimeter too wide, but it measured within the rules.

BY HELENE ST. JAMES

DENVER — When nothing else worked, the Avs accused Dominik Hasek of cheating. All it got them was a man in the penalty box and more great saves from Hasek.

After even Joe Sakic couldn't beat Hasek on two tries, the Avs opted to have Hasek's stick measured 23 seconds after they went on a second-period power play in Game 6. But the curves were perfect, and the height complied with NHL rule 20C, which dictates a maximum of 3½ inches.

Had either not complied, the Wings would have received a penalty. But the rule requires a penalty on the requesting team if no violation is found.

"We had information that Hasek was playing with an illegal stick," coach Bob Hartley said. "Sometimes in games you try some things that work. Unfortunately for us, that one didn't."

The information was gleaned from a stick Hasek gave Hartley when the Wings played at Colorado on Jan. 5. "He asked me for a stick for his son, so I gave him a stick," Hasek said. "It came from the factory. It may be one millimeter illegal."

Asked if he felt Hartley took advantage of him, Hasek nodded. "I think so," he said. "He was the one who had my stick."

ESPN's Barry Melrose didn't think much of Hartley's strategy. "It's a BS way to win," Melrose said between periods.

Not to split mullets, but it actually was a BS way to lose.

Believe!

A list of reminders was written in black marker on the white eraserboard in the Red Wings' dressing room before Game 6 — stuff like "backcheck" and "stay up" and "support the puck."

This was the last item: "No pressure, no diamonds."

To win a ring, you have to go through the wringer, and the Red Wings went through it in Game 6 of the Western Conference finals. They came out with a 2-0 victory over Colorado, winning their first elimination game in six years.

This also was written on the white eraserboard: "To accomplish great things, we must not only act, but also dream; not only plan, but also believe!"

The last word was underlined.

Nothing could be finer — bring on Carolina

MANDI WRIGHT

Red Wings encircled Tomas Holmstrom in a group hug after he scored the first of their seven goals in Game 7. Steve Duchesne, No. 28, and Luc Robitaille, No. 20, assisted on the goal.

BY MITCH ALBOM

Detroit's first shot was a goal, and Patrick Roy shook his head. Detroit's second shot was a goal, and Patrick Roy hung his head. Detroit's fifth shot was a goal, and Patrick Roy kicked the ice, flicked his neck, banged his stick, then skated away as if to leave.

Only one problem for the Colorado goalie and his soon-to-be-dethroned teammates:

There still were 2½ periods left. Now that's an avalanche. It rolled in off the Detroit River, it wore a red-and-white sweater, it skated as if its socks were on fire, and it scored one, two, three, four goals in the time it normally takes fans to find their seats. Then it scored five, six and seven.

It didn't merely rise to the

Au Rev-Roy

MANDI WRIGHT

1-0: Tomas Holmstrom (from Steve Duchesne, Luc Robitaille), 1:57 first period.

MANDI WRIGHT

2-0: Sergei Fedorov (from Steve Yzerman, Nicklas Lidstrom), 3:17 first period.

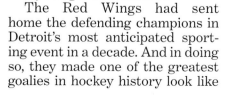

MANDI WRIGHT

3-0: Luc Robitaille (from Igor Larionov, Fredrik Olausson), 10:25 first period.

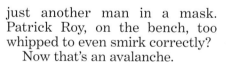

JULIAN H. GONZALEZ

5-0: Brett Hull (from Boyd Devereaux), 4:41 second period.

JULIAN H. GONZALEZ

4-0: Tomas Holmstrom (from Luc Robitaille, Igor Larionov), 12:51 first period.

JULIAN H. GONZALEZ

6-0: Fredrik Olausson (from Steve Yzerman, Nicklas Lidstrom), 6:28 second period.

JULIAN H. GONZALEZ

7-0: Pavel Datsyuk (from Brett Hull, Steve Duchesne), 16:09 third period.

occasion, it pole-vaulted, getting relentless offense, smothering defense, shutout goaltending and more jump than a 1956 Elvis Presley concert.

It was wild, voracious, a feeding frenzy in which everyone seemed to get to the trough. And at the final horn, for a brief but gloriously indulgent moment, everyone got to celebrate.

The Red Wings had sent home the defending champions in Detroit's most anticipated sporting event in a decade. And in doing so, they made one of the greatest goalies in hockey history look like

just another man in a mask. Patrick Roy, on the bench, too whipped to even smirk correctly?

Now that's an avalanche.

"To be honest, we thought this would be an overtime game," Steve Yzerman admitted after the Wings blew out the Avalanche, 7-0, to win Game 7 of the Western Conference finals and earn their first trip to the Stanley Cup finals since 1998. "After the first period, we were up, 4-0, and we were still thinking, 'This isn't how it's supposed to be.' "

In retrospect, Hoover Dam couldn't have held back Detroit.

Fueled by a knowledge that they had outplayed the Avalanche most of the series — yet still were in danger of losing it — the Wings poured gasoline on their personal fires, then added kerosene for good measure. It is almost easier to tell you who didn't score than who did.

First was Tomas Holmstrom, less than two minutes into the game, falling down while tangling with a defender but still redirecting a slap shot with his stick. Goal No. 1.

Then came Sergei Fedorov, 80 seconds later, flying down the left

Luc Robitaille got a hug from teammate Igor Larionov, right, after he scored the third goal of the Red Wings' four-goal first period against Patrick Roy and the Avalanche in Game 7.

MANDI WRIGHT

Our cup runneth over

Those Internet jokesters were at it again. The Freep received an e-mail playing off an ad that a radio station placed in Detroit and Denver papers: A photo composite — by an anonymous author — of Avs captain Joe Sakic holding aloft the cup.

OK, maybe not the Cup, but a cup.

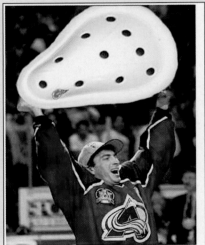

The only Cup coming back to Denver!

wing, lining up and firing one under Roy's arm. Goal No. 2.

Then it was Luc Robitaille, criticized for his lack of production, taking a pretty feed from Igor Larionov and flicking it cleanly between Roy's legs. Goal No. 3.

And here was Robitaille again, less than three minutes later, skating around three defenders — Luc Robitaille? Out-skating the Avalanche? — then firing point-blank on Roy. The rebound ricocheted out to a swooping Holmstrom, who put it home for a headshaking lead.

Four to nothing? After 13 minutes?

"Hey, Roy is one of the greatest goalies to ever play," said Brett Hull, who scored the Wings' fifth

PATRICK ROY BEFORE GAME 7

PATRICK ROY AFTER GAME 7

COLORAD'OH!

Free Press editorial cartoonist Mike Thompson gave fans the chance to stick it to Colorado goalie Patrick Roy by creating a Roy voodoo doll on the eve of the Western Conference finals. The two-sided cutout was to be filled with wadded-up tissue paper, taped together and stuck with pins whenever the Red Wings took a shot on Roy. Thousands of fans — including many who found the cartoon online — made their own dolls. Did the cumulative effects of their poking lead to Roy's Game 7 meltdown? Maybe, maybe not.

of the night, "but he's human, too."

So human, he ended the period without his stick, and he ended the game without his crown. This was more than a victory by Detroit, it was a proclamation, one they can post in big letters at Hockey's Town Hall:

Reputation is nothing.

Performance is everything.

You want an Avalanche?

That was an avalanche.

How sweet this was for Holmstrom, who had two goals in Game 7 but earned his glory night after night in the series, getting pounded and poked more than meat on a barbecue spit. Holmstrom did the dirtiest work in front of the net, but the most necessary to beat Colorado and Roy.

"Does this win make up for all the punishment?" he was asked.

"No," he said. "Winning the Cup will make up for it."

How sweet it was for Robitaille, who had to endure criticism because, on a team full of firepower, he had been firing blanks. Not in Game 7. Robitaille was all over the place, reminding fans why the Wings pursued him in the first place.

"You don't worry about how you're doing personally on this team," said Robitaille, who had a goal and two assists. "All you want to do is win. That's what makes it a special group."

How sweet for Brett Hull, who got one more shot at the finals. And how especially sweet for Dominik Hasek, who left Buffalo precisely for a moment like Game 7, a night when he outshone the biggest netminder in the game. Two shutouts in a row? Who's the Big Dog now?

How sweet for Yzerman, Larionov, Chris Chelios, Fredrik Olausson, Steve Duchesne — all the 35-and-older group who never

knew if they would get another shot at a Cup finals.

Sweet for all of them. And yes, let's say it, truly sweet for Detroit hockey fans, who — thank you, thank you, thank you — no longer had to hear about Colorado's amazing reputation for clutch performances.

There went Colorado, off to figure out what happened. There went Peter Forsberg, who had no shots in Game 7, and Joe Sakic, who had two. There, finally, went Roy, who skated next to last when the teams met for the postgame handshake.

Near the end of the line, Roy encountered Hasek and held out his hand. The symbolism was obvious. Roy had his helmet off. Hasek had his on — because he still had work to do.

Savor this, Detroit, a night to remember. You just saw an Avalanche defeated by an avalanche.

ON GUARD FOR 171 YEARS

Detroit Free Press

OAKLAND FINAL
35 cents

***
MONDAY
June 3, 2002

www.freep.com

DETROIT VS. CAROLINA
STANLEY CUP FINALS

Aunt Bee and Opie meet Hockeytown

Tobacco Road goes nuts over a sport on ice

By JEMELE HILL
FREE PRESS SPORTS WRITER

RALEIGH, N.C. — The first of June in North Carolina marks the start of hurricane season. But in Raleigh, the Hurricanes have been storming the region for weeks.

In an area crazy about college basketball and NASCAR, a fanatical new obsession called hockey — something we Michiganders know well — has been spawned.

And while the people of North Carolina admit they don't always understand what's going on — and some still call the puck a ball — their love for hockey has turned Raleigh and the surrounding cities known as the Triangle into Hockeytown of the South.

Many hockey pundits, especially Canadians, criticize Raleigh for its lack of hockey tradition and sophistication, and some refer to it as "Mayberry," the TV locale for "The Andy Griffith Show."

"So what?" said defenseman Aaron Ward, a former Red Wing. "I say, let's embrace it."

And the fans have, in many ways. The Hurricanes have become like rock stars. Their surprise appearance in the Stanley Cup finals against the Wings has not only turned the franchise — which five years ago was the Hart-

Please see CAROLINA, Page 5A

CHASING STANLEY

GAME 1: Tuesday at Detroit, 8 p.m. TV: ESPN, CBC (Channel 9 in Windsor).
● Come back to the Free Press on Tuesday for a special preview of the finals.

Even the small fry in North Carolina have big dreams about winning the Stanley Cup. Since moving from Hartford to Raleigh in 1997, the Hurricanes have steadily won over fans new to hockey.
DOUG PENSINGER/Getty Images

THE UNDERCOVER FAN | *Inside the playoff fan-demonium*

IN 1982: Mike and Marian Ilitch pose with their family outside Joe Louis Arena after buying the Red Wings. Clockwise from left: Carole, 14 at the time; Jim Lites (former son-in-law), 29; Atanas, 18; Mike Jr., 23; Chris, 17; Denise, 26; and Lisa, 22 (Ron isn't pictured).
PATRICIA BECK/Detroit Free Press

IN 1997: Red Wings owner Mike Ilitch celebrates his first Stanley Cup during a downtown parade that drew one million fans. His Wings won the Cup again in 1998. They are four victories from another, which would be the 10th in franchise history.
FRANCESCO KJOLSETH/Detroit Free Press

A date that will live in Red Wings lore

Ilitches bought storied franchise for $8 million

It was 20 years ago today. Led by patriarch Mike and matriarch Marian, the Ilitch clan marched into the limelight at a news conference at Joe Louis Arena on June 3, 1982. They were the new owners of the Red Wings.

"It was this team with an incredible history, and all of a sudden, we became the guardians of that. We were ecstatic," daughter Denise Ilitch said after the Wings had blown out the Avalanche on Friday to win the Western Conference championship.

The announcement was more important than anybody suspected. Fans hoped only that Ilitch would resuscitate the critically ill team and revive Detroit's dormant hockey fever.

No one knew the family would use the team as a launching pad to build a sports and entertainment empire and become key figures in restoring something else that was in critical condition — downtown Detroit.

As the Red Wings begin the Stanley Cup finals Tuesday night, attempting to win their third championship in six seasons, it is easy to forget how much has changed in two decades.

Mike, Marian and their seven children — three of whom were still teenagers when the family bought the team — have experienced both tremendous successes and bitter failures, and much of the drama has played out on the

Please see VAN, Page 10A

Clarissa and Erik Krefeld watch their 8-year-old son Raylee play at their newly purchased home in Detroit. More Michigan home owners spend at least 35 percent of their income on mortgages now.
Detroit Free Press

CENSUS: THE LONG FORMS

State felt 1990s boom; poverty falls

Data describes our homes, money, lives

By SHAWN WINDSOR
FREE PRESS STAFF WRITER

Detroit has shed the grim distinction it held a decade ago as the city with the highest percentage of families living below the U.S. poverty line, the latest census figures show.

Although poverty is still rampant in Detroit, its poverty rate ranked fourth among the nation's 10 largest cities during the 2000 Census. New Orleans, Miami and Cleveland rank above Detroit.

More broadly, the census also confirmed what many in Michigan already suspected: From Detroit to Troy, from River Rouge to the Upper Peninsula, prosperity grew in the 1990s.

Median household income, when adjusted for inflation, rose in all but 127 of Michigan's 1,776 cities, townships and villages.

"The 1990s were a sustained economic recovery," said Sheldon Danziger, the director of the Center for Poverty at the University of Michigan. "People who had a very hard time got work."

But the work is often a margin-al step above the poverty line, he said. The government defines poverty as a household income of less than $17,029 a year for a family of four.

Census officials today are providing the third major release of data from 2000. The numbers offer the first look at results from

the detail-rich long form sent to one in six households nationwide.

Among trends that stood out: the divorce rate stabilized in Michigan for the first time in decades. We spend increasingly large chunks of our income on housing. Women still earn less than men. We spend more time commuting than we did before. And we live farther and farther from urban centers.

The census also showed that we are becoming better educated, with a higher percentage of people in Michigan graduating from high school. It showed that Michi-

Please see CENSUS, Page 5A

THE LONG DRIVE TO WORK

Here is a comparison of average commute times for Detroit and the longest times within several surrounding counties in minutes:

	Longest	County average
DETROIT	28.4	
Highland Park	32.2	
Wayne County	25.8	
Oakland County	50.2	
Leonard		
Oakland County	24.6	
Armada Township	22.0	
Macomb County	24.3	
Manchester Township	34.1	
Washtenaw County	22.4	
Unadilla Township	36.5	
Livingston County	31	

Source: U.S. Census Bureau data, analysis by REGINAL TORRES/Detroit Free Press

Stakes can get high in MSU waiting game

Record 25,000 apply; late word could mean deposits are forfeited

By ERIK LORDS
FREE PRESS EDUCATION WRITER

For most of her life, Kim Piros wanted to attend Michigan State University. But by the time the Grosse Ile High School senior received her acceptance letter from MSU months later than she expected, she decided to go to Western Michigan University.

Piros, like about 1,000 other high school students who applied to MSU this school year, was not immediately accepted or rejected.

She was wait-listed.

MSU received 25,000 applications, a school record, for 6,800

slots in fall's freshman class, said Gordon Stanley, MSU's director of admissions.

Some students could still be waiting for an answer in late July — aka a record — MSU officials said. Until this year, the University of Michigan had been the only Michigan university to put so many students on hold for so long.

"It was horrible because I had to get things together for school — ships and grants and was kind of just waiting. I put $600 down at other schools, and I almost lost that."

Selective colleges across the nation, including MSU and U-M, annually place applicants on waiting lists as a hedge on how many

Please see MSU, Page 7A

INDEX

Bridge	2F	Crossword	6A	The List	3F
Classified		Editorials	10A	Lottery	2A
Comics	5F, 6F	Horoscope	2F	Movie Guide	7A
Corrections	2A	Metro	4B	Obituaries	7B

Sports 1E
TechToday 1C
Television 4F
The Way We Live 1F

CONTACT US

Delivery: 800-395-3300 Classified: 586-977-7500
News tips: 313-222-6600 800-926-8237

KNIGHT RIDDER

INFORMATION FOR LIFE

Even dog Carly got into the Red Wings spirit, along with Beverly Elementary crossing guard Mary Jo Hebert and fifth-grader Chris MacDonald in Beverly Hills.

DANGER AHEAD
STOP
REDWINGS COUNTRY

AMY LEANG

On the eve of the finals ...

IT WAS A HAPPY 20TH ANNIVERSARY FOR THE ILITCH FAMILY: Led by patriarch Mike and matriarch Marian, the Ilitch clan marched into the limelight at a news conference at Joe Louis Arena on June 3, 1982. They had become the new owners of the Red Wings. The price: $8 million.

At the time, the Wings had failed to make the playoffs for 14 of the previous 16 seasons. They had a bloated payroll of underachievers and has-beens, and one of the top executives was asking legendary general manager Jack Adams for advice. That was a problem, because Adams was dead — the executive was talking to his portrait.

"It was a very tough few years," daughter Denise Ilitch said. "I once said, 'Why couldn't we have bought the Islanders and started off a little higher up?' My dad said when you start at the bottom and you build your way up, it builds character and you appreciate it so much more. That's what we did. We built it up."

The team in 2002 was believed to be worth nearly $250 million.

DARREN McCARTY WAS THE LORD OF THE RINGS: "When you win it the first time, you're hungry to achieve something that you never have. It's a dream come true. It's the goal you had since you were a little kid. . . . Playing for the Stanley Cup. Winning the Stanley Cup. Drinking out of the Cup. Carrying the Cup. Getting a ring. Being a Stanley Cup champion.

"Then, when you do it back-to-back, you sort of spoil yourself. You say, 'Geez, man. How many years can I play? What's Henri Richard's record?' . . . Then, when you don't win it for a few years, you know what you're missing out on now."

McCarty keeps his rings in a safe, and he visited them when the Wings trailed Colorado, 3-2, in the Western finals: "I saw them the other day," he said. "They need another friend."

AND THE BATTLE LINES WERE BEING DRAWN — US VS. THEM:

Comparing the great states of Michigan and North Carolina:

We're Hockeytown. They're Tobacco Road.

We have the Stanley Cup. They have the Winston Cup.

We have places with car names, like Cadillac, Pontiac and Fairlane. They have places with cigarette names, like Raleigh, Winston-Salem and Asheville.

They have Barney Fife. We have Dugan Fife.

Our captain has grit. Their captain eats grits.

J. KYLE KEENER

The Finals

One for the books

BY NICHOLAS J. COTSONIKA

Scotty Bowman spoke to reporters and gave them a history lesson.

Dominik Hasek? Bowman compared his practice habits to Ken Dryden's.

Carolina's style? Bowman went back to the 1950s Canadiens and Henri Richard, who said their system for getting the puck out of their end was "as fast as we can."

Guys who've never won it all? Bowman brought up Red Wings great Bill Gadsby. "I saw him play," he said. "Never got his name on the Cup. Wasn't his fault."

He mentioned Bobby Orr and Jean Beliveau and, of course, Toe Blake.

Bowman recites history often because it isn't history to him. It's just who he is. In perhaps his best coaching performance since he arrived in Detroit in 1993, Bowman used his wealth of knowledge to win his ninth Cup as a coach, one more than Blake.

Asked beforehand about his chance to pass Blake, Bowman said, "I never worry about records." He said he would have been satisfied if he never had won another game after 1998, when he tied Blake, because "to even be thought of with Toe" was such an honor. He pointed out that Blake had won his eight Cups in 13 seasons and that 2001-02 was Bowman's 30th season. Blake, he said, "was far and way the best coach that's ever coached in the league."

Blake was Bowman's mentor. He taught him in the late 1950s to middle '60s, when he was coaching the powerful Canadiens and

Bowman was coaching the Canadiens' junior team.

At times, especially when he didn't think his team could win, Bowman could be aloof, detached, uninterested. The Wings had significant injuries during the 2001 playoffs. As they fell behind the Kings, Bowman withdrew. He didn't show up for practice the day before Game 6, in which the Wings were eliminated. But in 2002, Kris Draper said, "He's into it. He looks around the

dressing room and he sees a great situation."

The Wings had nine potential Hall of Famers. The players deserved most of the credit for their chemistry. But Bowman, who had been in the Hall of Fame for a decade, deserved some, too. People wondered whether anyone could balance all those egos, their ice time, their power-play time. "Well," Draper said, "he did it."

Steve Yzerman said Bowman was less hands-on than he used to

JULIAN H. GONZALEZ

Before passing Toe Blake with his ninth Stanley Cup as a coach, Scotty Bowman said "to even be thought of with Toe" was an honor. Blake mentored Bowman from the late '50s to middle '60s, when Blake coached the powerful Montreal Canadiens and Bowman coached its junior team.

be: "He'll just leave us alone at times." Said Brendan Shanahan: "He likes to step back and let the players put peer pressure on each other to get his message across."

When the coaches meet, ideas fly around the room like "Ping-Pong balls in a box," associate coach Dave Lewis said. But Bow-man always makes the final call. He is famous for doing the opposite of what a normal person would do. "If you figure him out, he's out of the game," Draper said. "Scotty wants to have that edge."

The day after the Wings took a 2-1 lead over Colorado in the third round, Bowman barked orders at practice. When the Wings were trailing, 3-2, he seemed in a good mood. When the series was tied, he pulled out his history.

As the Wings were dressing for warm-ups before Game 7, Bowman walked around the center of the room and told stories about his Game 7 experiences, dropping names like Glenn Hall. Here were all those potential Hall of Famers, listening like little kids, listening as they would to perhaps no other coach. He ribbed Draper about something. He got them laughing. He told them the game would be memorable no matter what happened, to just go out and do their best. They did. They went out and won, 7-0.

"He doesn't come in and give us big speeches," Shanahan said. "But certainly in big games and big moments, when you've got a guy that's been coaching as long as he has and can draw off his successes and experience, it can exude confidence to the players. I think he's one of those guys that if he believes it'll happen, that can rub off."

MANDI WRIGHT

Fredrik Olausson reached Ron Francis, left, too late: Francis had just scored the winner 58 seconds into overtime, redirecting the puck past a sprawled Dominik Hasek. "It was so fast," Hasek said. "All of a sudden, the puck was in the net."

Carolina time

BY NICHOLAS J. COTSONIKA

Yes, the Hurricanes upset the Red Wings in Game 1 of the Stanley Cup finals, 3-2. Fifty-eight seconds into overtime, Ron Francis — their lone answer to the Wings' nine potential Hall of Famers — redirected a pass past goaltender Dominik Hasek, and that was it. The Carolina franchise won at Joe Louis Arena for the first time since Nov. 14, 1989, when the Hartford Whalers beat the Wings, 3-0.

"I don't even know how it happened," Hasek said. "It was so fast. All of a sudden, the puck was in the net."

But the surprise wasn't how the Hurricanes played; it was how the Wings played. Whereas the Hurricanes stuck to the strict system that made them surprise Cup

Carolina's Tommy Westlund planted his elbow in the face of Tomas Holmstrom. The Hurricanes rallied from two one-goal deficits.

finalists, the Wings didn't do the little things that made them heavy favorites. They passed poorly. They stayed on the ice too long trying too hard to make something happen, and when they changed lines, they made mistakes. They didn't get the puck out of their end well enough. The list goes on.

"I didn't like our entire game," said Brendan Shanahan, who called the Hurricanes "patient" and the Wings "stupid." "We were sloppy. It's incredibly disap-

pointing. They played the kind of game you have to play in the Stanley Cup finals, and we didn't."

The Wings wasted plenty of opportunities.

Twice, they took a lead. Twice, the Hurricanes came back. Sergei Fedorov scored on the power play, then Sean Hill scored on a two-man advantage. Kirk Maltby scored, then Jeff O'Neill responded. "When you have a team down, you've got to finish them," Luc Robitaille said, "and we didn't."

The Wings failed to score on a power play in the final 1:41 of regulation and first 19 seconds of overtime. They finished 1-for-7. The Hurricanes went 1-for-6. "We scored a goal, but our power play could have made a difference," Shanahan said, "and I don't think it did."

As a result, the game went to overtime, which is Carolina time. The Hurricanes played a league-high 27 OT games in the regular season, and they were 6-1 in the playoffs before the finals. Only the 1993 Canadiens, who went 10-1 in OT on their way to the Cup, had won more OT games in a playoff season. The Wings were 1-3 in OT entering the finals.

"They were the better team," Shanahan said. "I don't think we disrespected them. I think we felt

It wasn't Dom's day

Everybody was scrambling for tickets, but Dominik Hasek got one he didn't want. Hasek was ticketed on the morning of Game I by Detroit Police for speeding in a construction zone on the Lodge Freeway.

Officer Alecia Thomas said Hasek was stopped on the southbound Lodge near Elizabeth around 10:30 a.m. for doing 65 in a 45-m.p.h. zone. Fines are doubled in construction zones, Thomas said, and Hasek's celebrity didn't get him off the hook.

"It doesn't matter who you are, if you're speeding in a construction zone, you will get fined," Thomas said. "It's not fair to give one person a ticket because of who they are and not the next person."

Former Free Press sports writer Joe Lapointe, writing for the New York Times, summed it up best: "Dominik Hasek's workday began with red lights flashing behind him, and it ended the same way."

coming in that they were playing great hockey. I think now everybody else is on board."

"We're not shocked to lose a game," Steve Yzerman said. "We're disappointed. We're in for a real battle. We have to play our best hockey."

Whew!

**BY NICHOLAS J. COTSONIKA
AND DREW SHARP**

First, Nicklas Lidstrom. Next, Kris Draper. Two goals in 13 seconds — the first with 5:08 left in the third period — and the Red Wings and their fans finally could exhale.

After shot after shot after shot hit a Hurricane or missed the net or found its way into goaltender Arturs Irbe, the Wings broke through and won, 3-1, tying the Stanley Cup finals at 1.

"Nick came to the rescue for us," Darren McCarty said. "If he hadn't, I don't want to think what might have happened if this game went into overtime with the way they're so successful in sudden death."

"We deserved to win this game because we played better in the second and third periods," said Dominik Hasek, who, midway through the third period, stoned Bates Battaglia in front of the net for the game's biggest save.

The Wings were much crisper, smarter and more patient against the Hurricanes' frustrating system than they were in Game 1. They almost doubled the Hurricanes in shots on goal, 30-17. They tripled them in shots attempted, 75-25.

"We could have scored a lot,

KIRTHMON F. DOZIER

Red Wings forward Brett Hull tried to slow down Bret Hedican in Game 2. Carolina coach Paul Maurice said the poor ice at Joe Louis Arena was "definitely, no question, a factor in the game."

but we didn't get the breaks," Mathieu Dandenault said. "But we stayed positive. You never give up, especially against this team."

The ice at Joe Louis Arena was so poor that Carolina coach Paul Maurice said "it was definitely, no question, a factor in the game." The Wings went 1-for-8 on the power play, the Hurricanes 0-for-8. Still, the Wings passed better. They also dumped in the puck better and forechecked better.

"We didn't play very well last game," associate coach Barry Smith said. "We didn't move the

puck fast enough. We didn't use the width of the ice. Tonight we started doing that, and we started having the defensemen skate the puck, which helped us tremendously. The forwards were in a better position."

Kirk Maltby and Carolina's Rod Brind'Amour traded short-handed goals in first period, and there was no scoring in the second period.

Kris Draper whiffed on a glorious chance about 1:10 into the third. A rebound popped into the low slot. Irbe was out of position.

Greetings from Mayberry

The Free Press previewed the Cup finals with a headline that proclaimed, "Aunt Bee and Opie Meet Hockeytown." After Game I, 'Canes fans shared their thoughts via e-mail:

● "We North Carolinians are not the hicks you Yankees portray us as. Anyway . . . Aunt Bee and Opie kicked ass last night."

● "It sure was silent in Hockeytown at the end

of the game last night. Now why is that? Regards, Andy Taylor."

● "Guess what? Mayberry just kicked your butt!"

● "You call that Hockeytown? I've heard more noise in a morgue. Wait till Game 3, and you'll hear how Opie and Aunt Bee can make noise."

● "Probably sucks to see Aunt Bee outplay all your Hall of Famers. I'd write more, but me and my sister are headin' to the spittin' contest. Later, y'all. Love, Opie."

● "Looks like Aunt Bee and Opie opened up a can of whoop-ass, huh?"

Strangely, no such e-mails arrived after Game 2.

Kris Draper exulted after scoring the Wings' third goal in their 3-1 win over the Carolina Hurricanes in Game 2. Darren McCarty skated in to join the celebration. Draper's goal came at 15:05 of the third period, 13 seconds after Nicklas Lidstrom scored to give the Wings a 2-1 lead.

The net was empty. Draper whirled around and backhanded the puck wide right.

Then the crowd got into it. One side of the rink yelled, "GO!" The other side yelled, "WINGS!" The volume was ear-splitting. Then the whole rink chanted, "LET'S GO, RED WINGS!"

"There were a couple of comments made on the bench about how loud it was," Draper said. "These fans want it just as bad as we do."

Then came the goals. From the right point on the power play, Lidstrom ripped a one-timer past Irbe's glove and into the upper right corner. Next, Draper took a pass from Lidstrom and fired from the left circle past Irbe's glove.

"Felt good," Draper said, "when McCarty gave me one of his patented big bear hugs there."

Stan the man

Would it be a bad omen?
Stanley Cupp lives in Raleigh.

"I have been picked on since I was 10 years old," said Cupp, a 53-year-old insurance auditor. "There's not a day goes by that I don't get some kind of comment.

"I use 'Stan' so people don't tie it to the Stanley Cup."

Cupp wasn't a hockey fan before the 'Canes came to town, but he said that's changing: "I'm still learning a lot about it. The first game I went to was awesome."

And he'd love to have another Stanley Cup in town. It's only fair, he says. "I've been looking to get back something for all the harassment I've been getting all these years," Cupp said.

But a bad omen? Nah.

BOB JORDAN/ASSOCIATED PRESS
Stanley Cupp goes by "Stan."

JULIAN H. GONZALEZ
Nicklas Lidstrom's winning goal in the third period had the Red Wings and their fans celebrating.

Nick of time

BY HELENE ST. JAMES

The easiest thing would have been to just leave Nicklas Lidstrom on the ice the entire game. Might as well save the poor guy the trouble of skating to the bench for his three-second breaks.

The Red Wings' $8.5-million defenseman, Norris Trophy-winner and monster-minute man rarely left the ice in Detroit's 3-1 win over the Hurricanes in Game 2. He played 34:38, scored the winning goal, set up the insurance goal and starred in every special-teams situation.

He one-timed the puck from the right circle on a power play late in the third period, breaking a 1-1 tie, then set up Kris Draper's goal 13 seconds later.

"He plays a smart game," Steve Yzerman said. "He knows what spots to be in, so I think he doesn't exhaust himself."

"He seems to have so much endurance," Scotty Bowman said.

"He has played great the whole season for us," Dominik Hasek said. "He is a very special player."

"I felt fine throughout the game," Lidstrom said. "I felt energized even late in the third period."

Whatever the situation, the Wings had an easy reaction: Send out the best. Send out Lidstrom.

Playoff payoff

MITCH ALBOM

It could've all been different. When the Red Wings and Hurricanes skated out for Game 3 in Raleigh — the first Stanley Cup final in North Carolina — it could've been reversed for Sergei Fedorov. He could've been on their side.

Fedorov, you'll recall, was offered a king's ransom to join the budding Carolina franchise in 1998. Peter Karmanos, the Detroit-born Hurricanes owner, loved the idea of signing Fedorov or, short of that, jacking up Mike Ilitch's payroll.

He succeeded at the latter. The Wings reluctantly matched the $38-million offer sheet, easily making Fedorov the team's highest-paid player at the time — but hardly its most popular.

"I remember those days well," Fedorov said. "During warm-ups at Joe Louis Arena, I would hear the people booing me."

He paused. Then he said something notable. "Maybe I deserved some of it."

Hmm. I can't tell you everything about Sergei Fedorov, but I can tell you this: He wouldn't have said that in 1998.

Fedorov, for my money, was the Wings' most consistently excellent player in the playoffs. He flew on the ice. He played huge minutes. He was a swingman for the Wings whenever injury or fatigue plagued other forwards. He killed penalties, he shadowed attackers, he led rushes into the other team's zone and, as if that weren't enough, he scored huge goals when Detroit most needed them.

GABRIEL B. TAIT

The Red Wings might've paid a hefty price to keep forward Sergei Fedorov from Carolina in 1998, but his stellar play against the Hurricanes in 2002 helped justify the expense.

Remember those white skates Fedorov used to wear? He still has them.

"They are in my museum," he said. You have a museum?

"Well, my basement. I keep stuff there."

Museum. Basement. What's the difference? The fact is, those white skates, part of a huge Nike campaign, were the kind of thing that made Fedorov stand out or, worse, look like he was trying to stand out.

He doesn't wear them now. He looks the same as the other Red Wings — except he often skates faster and is more effective.

Let's face it. It is a joy to watch Fedorov play. Even his critics admit that. The fluidity, the skating prowess, the crisp passing — and now, more and more, the defense.

"I would like to be able to play well enough to be considered again for the Selke Trophy (for best defensive forward, which he won in 1994 and 1996). I want to prove to myself that I can still be good at both ends."

After he re-signed with Detroit, Fedorov found Ilitch and quietly assured him, "I will earn every penny."

The ledger sheet is quickly balancing.

Morning glory

BY NICHOLAS J. COTSONIKA

RALEIGH, N.C. — After 114 minutes and 47 seconds of hockey, after winning a 3-2, triple-overtime thriller, after taking a 2-1 lead over Carolina in the Stanley Cup finals, the Red Wings finally went to bed.

And stayed awake awhile.

"You're just lying there," Kris Draper said. "Your body's asleep, but you're not."

"Your mind is racing," Kirk Maltby said. "You're thinking about all the things that happened in the course of the game. It's hard to get to sleep when you're thinking about that kind of stuff. You're telling yourself to sleep, sleep, sleep. But every time you try to stop thinking about it, you just think about it more."

This was a classic. It was the third-longest finals game in history. Twenty-seven seconds more, and it would have been the longest.

With less than two minutes left in regulation, the Wings trailed, 2-1, and their karma was bad. Steve Yzerman had hit the left post midway through the first period. Steve Duchesne had hit the right post early in the third.

Still, they had confidence.

"You have got so many great players and so many guys that can score goals, you never feel like you are out of it," Brett Hull said.

Yzerman won a draw in the right circle. Sergei Fedorov passed from the right point to the left. Nicklas Lidstrom took a shot, and Hull — holding out his stick in the slot — tipped the puck past goaltender Arturs Irbe.

One minute, 14 seconds remained.

Hull said the play might have been "dumb luck," but Brendan

MANDI WRIGHT

Igor Larionov sent the puck past Carolina goaltender Arturs Irbe in the third overtime, ending the third-longest Stanley Cup finals game in history.

Numbers game

Crunching the Red Wings-Hurricanes triple-overtime Game 3:

8:14 p.m.: Time of opening face-off.

1:14: Time left in regulation when Brett Hull tied the score at 2 and forced overtime.

1:15 a.m.: Time of day when Igor Larionov scored in the third overtime for a 3-2 victory — 5 hours, 1 minute after the game started.

114:47: Playing time in minutes and seconds.

1: Players who were on the ice the entire time — 'Canes goalie Arturs Irbe. Dominik Hasek was off 25 seconds on delayed penalties.

52:03: Ice time logged by Nicklas Lidstrom, the iron man among skaters (Carolina's Bret Hedican was second with 49:34 and Chris Chelios third with 46:38).

9:28: Least ice time of any player, the Hurricanes' Kevyn Adams. Pavel Datsyuk was the Wings' low man with 19:48.

.948: Combined save percentage by Hasek (.953) and Irbe (.943).

.979: Combined save percentage in overtime by Hasek (1.000) and Irbe (.958).

96: Shots taken in the game — 53 by the Wings, 43 by the Hurricanes.

46: Shots taken in overtime — 24 by the Wings, 22 by the 'Canes.

26: Face-offs taken by Steve Yzerman — he won 17.

3: Shots taken in the game by Larionov.

2: Goals scored by Larionov.

Wings goaltender Dominik Hasek was on the bottom of this pileup after Brendan Shanahan (14) hit Carolina's Martin Gelinas in the first overtime. Shanahan had a chance to win the game in that period, one-timing a pass from Sergei Fedorov on a 2-on-1. He sent the puck inches left of an open net.

Shanahan said Hull had such awesome hand-eye coordination that it was "not an accident he got his stick on it."

Regardless, the score was tied, and Hull said the Hurricanes must have been saying, "Oh, my God."

Lidstrom hit the left post with 50 seconds left in regulation. Yzerman cut in on goal with one second left.

OVERTIME I

The chances kept coming. About 8:35, Pavel Datsyuk made Gretzky-like moves — stickhandling past forward Sami Kapanen, then defenseman Marek Malik — but Irbe got his left pad on the puck. About 12:44, one-timing a pass from Fedorov on a 2-on-1, Shanahan fired inches wide left of a yawning net.

Shanahan shook his head on the bench.

"Good thing I didn't have a knife," Shanahan said, "or I would've slit my throat."

About 15:35, Fredrik Olausson hit the crossbar.

The host Carolina Hurricanes weren't the only ones with their mouths agape after Red Wings forward Brett Hull scored with 1:14 remaining in regulation, tying the game at 2 and sending it to overtime. "You have so many great players and so many guys that can score goals, you never feel like you are out of it," Hull said.

"You start to wonder if it's ever going to go in," Olausson said.

OVERTIME II

The Hurricanes killed a penalty. Then the Wings killed one, although Dominik Hasek made things interesting by wandering from his net and falling.

Yzerman had the best scoring chance about 16:39. At the end of a pretty passing play, Shanahan sent the puck from the right wing across the slot. Yzerman put it on net, but Irbe dived and snagged it with his glove. Yzerman rolled head over heels, then appeared to swear and say, "I don't believe it!"

Said Shanahan: "I was thinking, 'Well, at least I'm not the only guy.'"

OVERTIME III

In the Carolina dressing room, players were taking fluids intravenously. In the Detroit dressing room, things were relatively routine.

"I have always thought that youth and enthusiasm will take you only so far," Hull said. "I said to Iggy after the game, 'I'd rather be old and smart than young and dumb any day.'...

"I think that really helps us because when you are in a tight situation, you come in between periods and Steve Yzerman is talking like he's about to fall asleep. He's so calm. But his words just ring loud."

Carolina forward Jaroslav Svoboda had a chance early.

"I was kind of holding my breath a little bit there," Yzerman said.

As the period went on, both teams were trying to catch their breath.

"Everybody was feeling it a little bit," Yzerman said. "It was basically one burst of energy and head right to the bench."

And in the end, the NHL's oldest player had the jump in his legs

to end it.

Igor Larionov, the 41-year-old center, took a pass from Tomas Holmstrom on the rush. He stick-handled past diving defender Bates Battaglia. Then, with Mathieu Dandenault in front, he backhanded the puck over Irbe and into the roof of the net at 14:47.

"I think this is the biggest goal of my career," said Larionov, who never had scored a playoff overtime goal and became the oldest player ever to score in the finals. "It's obviously huge for me."

It was 1:15 in the morning.

"We're the oldest team in the league, and we had the oldest player go out and dance around a couple of guys like it was the first shift of the game," Shanahan said. "It's just a big relief to our entire team. We had so many chances that I think relief was part of the feeling."

The Wings celebrated. The full impact of fatigue didn't hit them until they were on the bus or back at the hotel. They had a meal about 2 a.m.

"We weren't even sure if the hotel was going to keep the food for us, but they did," Draper said.

They ate pasta, pizza, chicken, salads — all kinds of stuff.

"The food was meant to be eaten about two or three hours earlier," Maltby said. "It was actually not bad."

How was the atmosphere?

"Pretty quiet," Draper said.

"And content," Olausson said.

One by one, the players went to their rooms and tried to unwind.

"Some guys I'm sure had a beer," Maltby said.

Maltby turned off his television, tossed and turned for about a half hour or 45 minutes, then fell asleep between 4:30 and 5. Yzerman didn't fall asleep until after 5.

"It was a lot of fun to be involved in that game," Maltby said, "but it's really tiring."

Come fill the Cup

The five-hour marathon game took its toll on many of the younger Hurricanes. Some needed to replace fluids intravenously during intermission after the second overtime.

As for the elder statesmen Gray Wings, they dined on bananas and oranges. And in perhaps the funniest twist, the magic mixture for the older team was a children's drink that replaces important minerals lost when a youngster is fighting the effects of diarrhea.

Pedialyte: The official drink of the Stanley Cup champions.

Think of the marketing possibilities.

"Hi, I'm Igor Larionov. And when my teammates and I run out of Geritol, we drink Pedialyte. It's great for the long run, as well as for a case of the runs."

Why not a standard sports drink? Wings trainer John Wharton said there are more electrolytes in the little kids' drink and a faster rate of absorption.

"I've given it to my little girl when she's gotten sick," Kris Draper said. "And now we've found another use for it. It's strange how these things work out. But if we should win the Stanley Cup, maybe we should pour Pedialyte in there before any champagne."

By Drew Sharp

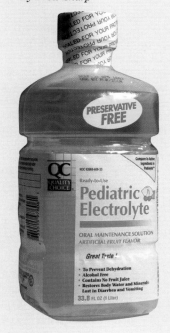

MITCH ALBOM

Ask the Professor

In hockey, as in life, the difference between the old and the young is patience — only in hockey, the young have more of it.

"They think 'We have time, we can grow, losing is not so bad,'" said Igor Larionov, the oldest player in the NHL. "An older team says, 'We cannot waste this chance. We have to do it now.'"

That was the feeling as the Red Wings began the last leg of their last waltz, the Stanley Cup finals. Make no mistake, if they didn't win it all, this veteran team — maybe the best roster in NHL history — would not be back. Dominik Hasek, arguably the most irreplaceable man on the roster, could retire. Others could be cut for expenses. Others could slow with age and injury.

"Do you think, if you win the Cup, you should go out on the high note?" I asked Larionov.

"That's a very good question," he said. "So it requires some thought. I will think about it after the season is over, in my house in Florida. I will have maybe a glass of wine, sit by the pool, talk about it with my family."

Wait a minute. Did he say a glass of wine? In Florida? By a pool?

What, no shuffleboard?

Well. He was 41 years old. He was also symbolic of this Red Wings team: They may not all have been drinking wine by the pool, but they weren't hosting kegger parties, either. This was a team so top-heavy with experience that nine of its players were older than the Carolina Hurricanes' coach. The Wings had 40-year-old Chris Chelios, 37-year-olds Steve Yzerman, Brett Hull and Dominik Hasek, 36-year-olds Luc Robitaille, Steve Duchesne

and Uwe Krupp, and 35-year-old Fredrik Olausson.

And then there was Larionov. He deserved special mention — a medical marvel, an anathema to aging, a wrinkle-free face and hair that seemed to have been washed with Johnson's Baby Shampoo. He was the oldest man still standing in the playoffs. He was the oldest in the entire league. His nickname was neither Bubba nor Bammer nor Jammer nor Crash.

It was "The Professor."

And though most of these Red Wings pointed to Yzerman, the Captain, as their inspiration and role model, the Captain often pointed to Larionov as a guy he looked up to.

You want to know why a Stanley Cup meant so much to these Detroit players?

Consider one man's story.

Raised in the small Russian town of Voskresensk, Igor Larionov was coached by a Jewish man who, unable to work with the biggest and strongest, had to develop the bodies he had. Larionov, barely 5-feet-9, learned to be smart as well as strong. He was quick. He passed well. He was chosen, as a teenager, over bigger, stronger players for the Soviet elite team. And soon he joined the Red Army team, renowned as the best of the best.

"We had one day off per year," he said. "And we trained three times a day. One of the drills we had there was to run laps around a (quarter-mile) track. And you had to do 12 in a row under 70 seconds."

He paused.

"And if you couldn't do it anymore, you were considered too old to be a hockey player."

Larionov shook his head. He

knew that were he still under that system, he'd have been out of the game. That mentality, with the rigid "these-are-our-rules-and-don't-you-question-them" Soviet system, was one factor that eventually drove Larionov to seek other pastures.

That journey eclipsed any story from the finals. Larionov had to fight against a dictatorial Soviet

Igor Larionov — not only the oldest Red Wing but, at age 41, also the NHL's most senior citizen — was the center of attention after scoring the winner in triple overtime of Game 3. Youngsters Steve Duchesne (age 36) and Mathieu Dandenault (26) helped Larionov celebrate Detroit's victory.

coaching staff — even as he was leading teams to world championships and Olympic gold medals. He had to fight to get his release to leave the country. Even when he came to the NHL in 1989, he had to fight to keep a fair share of his money. At one point, he went to Switzerland to play because of the Soviet Union's interference with his contracts.

Here was a man who, at some point in his life, left a country, a culture, a team, a society, his friends, his family, his language and his mentors — all for the chance to play for the Stanley Cup.

In Game 3 and throughout the finals, Larionov did not waste his chance.

Bring it home

BY MITCH ALBOM

RALEIGH, N.C. — It was only a number. It was only one shot. And Brett Hull had taken a million shots in nearly two decades in this league. But there he was in the Cup finals, taking a beautiful feed from Boyd Devereaux, dropping to one knee and firing away. The "ping" off the post was like a magic password that opened the trap door. The puck ricocheted into the net, a secret tree house appeared, and Hull climbed into a very exclusive club.

It was only a number, but what a number, his 100th goal in the playoffs, a mark reached by only three other men. Hull made history, all right. But it wasn't history that made him leap into his teammates' arms. It was the 1-0 lead he provided. It was the small push of this piano-heavy force that they were collectively trying to shove across the finish line.

"How did it feel, joining that club?" someone asked Hull after the electric 3-0 victory over Carolina that moved the Red Wings to within one triumph of the Stanley Cup.

"Well, it's amazing to think about the people I've joined," he said, referring to Wayne Gretzky,

JULIAN H. GONZALEZ

Brendan Shanahan put the finishing touch on goaltender Arturs Irbe and the Hurricanes, scoring the Red Wings' final goal at 14:43 of the third period.

THE FINALS

Carolina's Ron Francis (10) and Bates Battaglia converged on Dominik Hasek in the second period, but the goaltender made the save. He stopped all 17 shots he faced, and picked up his sixth shutout of the playoffs.

'It had to be done'

From left, Frank Ciavattone, Harry Wilson and Scott Legas showed they keep the memory of past Red Wings Cups near and dear to their hearts.

MANDI WRIGHT

BY MICHAEL ROSENBERG

RALEIGH, N.C. — Late in the third period of Game 4, with the Red Wings leading, 3-0, Harry Wilson Jr. stood on the concourse outside Section 115 of the Entertainment and Sports Arena. He wore his red Chris Chelios jersey.

Other Wings fans who made the trip here were celebrating. Wilson was not. "I just want to know what happened to my brother," he said as he leaned against a post. "I just want to make sure he's OK."

Mike Wilson had come down from his third-level seat, slipped past the Section 115 security guard and walked down until he found an open seat next to other Wings fans. Then he whispered his secret.

"I," he said, "have got an octopus."

At the next stoppage in play, Mike scooted down toward the ice and let go a pass that would've made Joey Harrington jealous. The octopus landed right in front of Hurricanes goalie Arturs Irbe.

He shoots, he scores!

But as he walked back to his seat, Mike was jumped by a half-dozen or so 'Canes fans, who promptly started beating him.

Harry, 34, and Mike, 25, were fourth-generation firefighters for the Detroit Fire Department. They were used to dangerous missions. They didn't think this would be one of them.

As the stands emptied, Harry still couldn't find his brother. He asked security guards. He asked cops. He walked around the concourse. Finally, when he learned that Mike had definitely not been arrested, Harry walked out of the arena with his father and a couple of friends.

That's where they found Mike, in the West parking lot, leaning against their white pickup truck with the "Livonia Hockey" sticker in the back window. He was sipping a beer and feeling giddy.

"They couldn't have given me a bruise that I'd feel right now," Mike said. "If they'd broken my arm, I'd be out here right now, celebrating. An octopus on the ice! It had to be done."

The Wilsons said that just about everybody else in Raleigh had been incredibly nice to them. They weren't about to let a few bitter fans spoil their opinion of the place.

And as far as they were concerned, Mike was some sort of hero.

"The real heroic thing," said Harry Sr., "was how he sat with the octopus for the whole game. That thing really stunk."

Mark Messier and Jari Kurri. "But on this team, if you don't get one goal or if you get five, it's the same as long as you win."

He smiled. "You know, there was a time when people said you couldn't win a Stanley Cup with Brett Hull on your team, and — "

"Wait," interjected Brendan Shanahan, who was sitting nearby. "Did you just refer to yourself in the third person?"

"I was trying to give myself a pat on the back."

"Oh, OK. If you have 100 playoff goals you can do that."

They both laughed. A team.

So there they were, returning home on the wings of three straight victories in the finals. Hull's special number was indeed just part of his team's story. And Hull, a guy who, incredibly, was unsigned and barely pursued after the 2000-01 season, continued his run as a mature force at critical junctures. He had a hat trick to

Century club

Brett Hull scored his 100th playoff goal in Game 4 of the Cup finals, becoming the fourth player in NHL history to reach 100. The top five playoff goal-scorers (with GP-games played and G-goals):

PLAYER	GP	G
Wayne Gretzky	208	122
Mark Messier	236	109
Jari Kurri	200	106
Brett Hull	186	100
Glenn Anderson	225	93

MANDI WRIGHT

Brett Hull, left, hugged Boyd Devereaux after his 100th career playoff goal gave the Wings a 1-0 lead.

JULIAN H. GONZALEZ

Kris Draper stumbled to the ice after getting hooked by Carolina defenseman Glen Wesley at 2:05 of the first period. The Red Wings were unable to convert on the power play, but no matter, they still scored three at even strength.

close out the Vancouver series. He had six points against Colorado. He had a huge goal late in Game 3 against Carolina to save the Wings from defeat.

That deflection, near the end of regulation, took the life out of the Hurricanes and their noisy crowd. They were still smarting during Game 4 when Hull did it again, 6½ minutes into the second period.

It was only a number. It was just one shot.

One big, big shot.

And for Dominik Hasek, it was also only a number. A zero on the scoreboard. A shutout — his sixth of the playoffs. But this one had resonance. This was like a war cry, heard throughout the whole of North Carolina, because Hasek had only gotten stronger as the postseason rolled on.

There he was in Game 4, making sharp saves, making hard saves, getting lucky when he needed luck, being good when he needed good. He stopped all 17 of the Carolina shots, a virtual plug in the net.

"Do you feel like you're getting stronger?" Hasek was asked after the shutout.

"No stronger," he said, "but just as strong as when I started. I am not doing anything different.

"And I do not want to do anything different."

It was only a number. It was only one shutout.

But, man, what a time for a shutout.

"Now it's just a matter of staying away from the hoopla," Scotty Bowman said. "As soon as this game was over, our guys were warning each other. You go home and your good friends and your relatives, and they're all well-meaning and they want to be there when you win — but that doesn't help you play.

"We have to shut that down."

One shot. One shutout. One game. They were all just numbers, but numbers add up. And if you collect them just right, they turn to letters.

And the letters spelled "G-L-O-R-Y."

The players didn't say it, but the rest of us did. Get ready. You could feel that glory, on the wings of a red-and-white airplane, coming home and planning to stay.

OCTOMETER

Observations on Game 4 of the finals (rated on a scale of one to four octopi):

 Well, a 3-1 lead sounds pretty good, doesn't it? But let's not get ahead of ourselves — they always say the fourth victory is the toughest. Wow. Weren't the first three tough enough?

 Not that he gets burned, but doesn't it make you nervous when Dominik Hasek keeps wandering out of his net? Maybe they should make him pay roaming charges.

 It's about time the pipes cooperated, after four Wings shots clanked off them in Game 3. This time, they denied Ron Francis and let Brett Hull bank in the winner. Heck, even Shanny sneaked one in.

I'll pick Nick

DREW SHARP

He was tireless, patient, as smooth in a locker room of superstars as in his own defensive zone.

But soft-spoken Nicklas Lidstrom was too modest to spout his virtues. So permit me.

The man won the Conn Smythe Trophy, a tribute to playoff consistency as much as excellence. And he earned it.

He earned it as the Red Wings snuffed out the Carolina Hurricanes with a customary suffocating defense. He earned it with his headline-worthy goals. He earned the recognition from others he declined to give himself.

"I don't think about those things," he said when a reporter futilely tried coaxing a little self-acknowledgment from the Swede. "You can't lose sight of the team objective."

Lidstrom became the first European to win the Conn Smythe (or should that be the Cann Smythe, since the only previous non-Canadian winner in its 38-year history was American Brian Leetch, who won it with the New York Rangers in 1994).

"We're a team of great players," Wings forward Kirk Maltby said, "with guys who are very valuable. But you look at these playoffs, and the guy we could least afford to lose for an extended period of time would be Nick. And that's because he logs so much time."

Lidstrom played more than 52 minutes of the triple-overtime thriller that was Game 3, and he averaged 30-plus minutes through the playoffs. He quietly left huge footprints throughout this cham-

J. KYLE KEENER

Players and fans alike kept their eyes on superstar defenseman Nicklas Lidstrom throughout the playoffs. The defending Norris Trophy winner played more than 30 minutes a game, scored some key goals and set up a few more.

pionship march.

There were several other Red Wings who were deserving candidates for the Conn Smythe, such as Dominik Hasek, Steve Yzerman, Brett Hull and Sergei Fedorov.

But Lidstrom best symbolized the defensive stability that made playoff life relatively easy for Hasek and the rest.

"You can't just look at one person and say that's why we've played well," Lidstrom said. "The credit goes all around. Cheli (Chris Chelios) was healthy all season and had a great year. ... Freddie (Olausson) and Stevie (Duchesne) were consistent all season and the young guys like Jiri (Fischer) stepped up with big contributions."

Thus it was somewhat ironic that a team assembled for its offensive prowess won the Stanley Cup primarily because of its defensive stinginess. Hasek's save

percentage wasn't even ranked in the top five among playoff goalies, but it didn't have to be. Funny, isn't it? He was brought into town to compensate for perceived defensive shortcomings.

"This was the best defense I've ever had in front of me," Hasek said. "I don't want to say that it takes the pressure off the goalie, but it makes you feel more comfortable.

"Knowing that I'll have guys like Lidstrom and Chelios out there for a combined total of 50 minutes for each game helps you. There have been times in these playoffs where I haven't gotten much work because the defense wasn't giving up many good scoring chances."

The Wings' defense reflected the attitude of its leader. Its efficiency might have been underappreciated, but it won the ultimate reward.

Eyes on the prize

What some of the Wings were saying before Game 5

J. KYLE KEENER

The heat was on Brendan Shanahan, Sergei Fedorov, Brett Hull and Steve Yzerman to clinch the Stanley Cup in Game 5. But the veterans — all potential Hall of Famers, all past Cup winners — stayed cool, calm and collected in the days leading up to the game.

Brendan Shanahan

"There has been pressure on this team all year long and we have all kind of shouldered it equally. It has been that way with each round. It's that way today. It's that way until we do accomplish our goal."

Sergei Fedorov

"You have to glue together. And, basically, you can't really enjoy it and relax until it is over."

Brett Hull

"Just go out and make sure you stay focused, but also relax and free yourself from a little bit of emotion and stress for a day, a day and a half, maybe."

Steve Yzerman

"We can't lose our edge, lose any kind of focus and expect that it will be an easy game. As long as we're prepared to play a tough game, we will be OK."

PHOTO NEXT PAGE BY J. KYLE KEENER

The crowd in the Joe was roaring: "We want the Cup!" And Brendan Shanahan's second goal of the game, into an empty net with 44.5 seconds left, gave the fans what they wanted. The scoreboard had yet to reflect the final score, 3-1.

THE FINALS

Thanks, Scotty

BY NICHOLAS J. COTSONIKA

The final horn sounded, the confetti fell, and as the Red Wings celebrated the 3-1 victory over Carolina that brought them the Stanley Cup, Scotty Bowman skated onto the ice. He found owner Mike Ilitch amid the throng, gave him a hug and whispered something in his ear.

"What he said in my ear was, 'Mike, it's time. The time is right now,'" Ilitch said. "'It's time to go.'"

And so, after three Cups in six seasons, after a record nine Cups as a coach, after setting every other coaching record there was to set, Bowman skated off into the sunset. When NHL commissioner Gary Bettman handed the Cup to Steve Yzerman, the Captain handed it right to Bowman, and Bowman took a victory lap around the ice, holding it high.

"What a way for the greatest coach in the history of the sport to exit," general manager Ken Holland said.

"He did an incredible job with all these egos and high-profile players," Holland said. "He got them all to buy into the team concept. He's the master. It's a team that I'll never forget, and I'm sure a lot of fans will never forget."

"It's bittersweet," Brett Hull said. "To go out like this and to have the success he's had is so wonderful, but then to have it end is so sad. I feel as fortunate as anybody alive to say that he was my coach."

Said Brendan Shanahan: "I was shocked. He's been so involved and so excited throughout the whole playoffs that I just thought the way he was responding, this guy's going to go forever. But I guess it makes sense now.

THE FINALS

Players on the bench beamed with joy as Game 5 of the Stanley Cup finals — and their successful quest for the Red Wings' 10th Cup — ended.

KIRTHMON F. DOZIER

Lucky stars

Before Game 5, before they clinched the Cup, a couple of Red Wings revealed their superstitious sides.

LUC ROBITAILLE

The opportunity had presented itself on a number of occasions for Robitaille, who had made many friends during his 16-year NHL career. A few of those friends had earned the privilege of keeping company with the Stanley Cup.

But Robitaille rebuffed each offer. Thanks, but no thanks. No posing beside the Cup, no pictures taken of him holding it. He didn't want to be in the same room with it because he had too much respect for what it symbolized: The dream of every boy who ever put on a pair of skates.

"I haven't earned the honor yet," Robitaille said, before he had. "The players who have their names on it went through a lot to get there. Out of appreciation for what it takes, I don't think a player should be around it until he can say he's won it."

By Drew Sharp

JULIAN H. GONZALEZ

Luc Robitaille enjoyed his Cup moment with his family.

DOMINIK HASEK

No, he said. He would not go onstage. He would stand near it. He would stand in front of it. But he would not go up on it. Superstition. No stages. And Hasek would not budge.

So the reporters in the Joe Louis Arena news conference had to leave their seats and swarm to encircle him at ground level. Half of them ended up on the same stage Hasek refused to ascend, poking cameras over his back and tape recorders over his head. It was a hot, uncomfortable crush. Silly, really. But the message was clear:

He had gotten this far doing it his way. He wasn't going to change.

"One day I will take the stage," promised Hasek, the oldest player on the Red Wings who had never won a Stanley Cup. "But not while we are still playing. There is still one more win we must get."

By Mitch Albom

THE FINALS

He knew it was his last playoff, and that's why he soaked it all up."

No fewer than five Wings were legitimate candidates for the Conn Smythe Trophy as the playoffs' most valuable player: Dominik Hasek, Yzerman, Sergei Fedorov, Hull and Nicklas Lidstrom. In the end, Lidstrom won. "It's a wonderful tribute to him," Bowman said.

But everyone contributed, from the greats to the grinders. In the clincher, Shanahan scored two goals, and Tomas Holmstrom — perhaps the grittiest grinder of them all — pitched in another.

"There's no better feeling," Hasek said.

The crowd was loud as the team took the ice. "LET'S GO, RED WINGS!"

But after a scoreless first period, they were quiet at the start of the second. Then Holmstrom woke up the joint at 4:07. From the corner to goalie Arturs Irbe's left, Igor Larionov passed the puck into the slot. Charging ahead of a defender, lunging with one hand on his stick, Holmstrom deflected the puck between Irbe's legs. Holmstrom crashed into the end boards.

As he lay on his back, he pumped his fists skyward. The goal was his eighth of the playoffs. He had eight goals during the regular season. "LET'S GO, RED WINGS!"

Shanahan gave the Wings a 2-0 lead on the power play at 14:04. Low in the right circle, he one-timed a pass from Fedorov off Irbe and high into the net. He smiled as the fans danced to his Irish jig. "LET'S GO, RED WINGS!"

At 18:50, Jeff O'Neill cut the Wings' lead on the power play. With forward Erik Cole in front of Hasek, who held a teammate's stick because he had lost his own, O'Neill shot from the left wing. The puck hit the back of the net and bounced out so quickly that the officials needed a lengthy delay to review the video and confirm the goal.

Dominik Hasek, one of five legitimate candidates for the Conn Smythe award as playoff MVP, held the Hurricanes scoreless in the third period with five saves.

JULIAN H. GONZALEZ

Sergei Fedorov flew down the ice on a breakaway during the scoreless first period. Fedorov set up Brendan Shanahan's winning goal in the second period.

JULIAN H. GONZALEZ

Reserve defenseman Jiri Slegr got the call to play in Game 5 when Jiri Fischer was suspended, then made one of his own on a cell phone as teammates celebrated in the locker room.

"Obviously it gives them a great boost going into the third period," Shanahan said during the second intermission. "We have to respond, and we know we can."

With 9:19 left, television cameras caught white-gloved men taking the Cup out of its crate backstage. The Wings kept skating, banging, chipping the puck out of their zone, chipping it ahead, waiting to exhale. "LET'S GO, RED WINGS!" With about 7:35 left, Yzerman nearly scored. With about 7:13 left, Holmstrom had a chance. With 4:43 left, an octopus hit the ice in front of Hasek. The Joe roared.

And roared. And roared. Holmstrom had a chance. Then Fedorov. "WE WANT THE CUP!" With 45 seconds left, they had it. From just across the red line, right in front of the Carolina bench, Shanahan fired the puck into an empty net. He leapt for joy. His teammates leapt with him. All season, they said they wouldn't celebrate until their job was done. Now it was.

"We were too old, too slow, too rich — fat cats," said Barry Smith, Bowman's longtime associate coach. "That's what we were told, and these guys were unbelievable. They sacrificed an awful lot, each one of these guys. They sacrificed ice time. They sacrificed personal power plays. They sacrificed a lot of things to make this a team.

"They fought hard all season. They won the Presidents' Trophy as the best team all year, and they won the Stanley Cup. What else can you ask for? There's nothing else to win. They won it all."

He taught them how to win

TOP PHOTO AND PHOTO ON FOLLOWING PAGE BY JULIAN H. GONZALEZ

**Above: Coach Scotty Bowman and owner Mike Ilitch embraced after the Wings' Game 5 clincher.
Next page: Brett Hull helped with the hardware as Scotty Bowman prepared for a final drink
from the Stanley Cup — his record ninth as a coach.**

**DREW
SHARP**

Steve Duchesne dropped what teeth he had left when the stunning announcement filtered through the celebration on the Joe Louis Arena ice.

"Scotty leaving?" Duchesne said with an incredulous look. "What? When? Why?"

Those were the precise questions everyone had when Scotty Bowman turned a Stanley Cup coronation into a farewell waltz with the trophy he has won more than any other coach.

Bowman told associate coach and good friend Barry Smith of his decision to retire just before the start of the decisive Game 5. He didn't tell anyone else until the Red Wings took the ice for the trophy presenta-

tion. He approached owner Mike Ilitch, who brought Bowman to town in 1993, and gave him a hug, whispering in his ear: "Mike, it's time. It's time to go."

That was the last thing Ilitch expected to hear.

Bowman then went over to the player he molded into the consummate team leader, Steve Yzerman. The Captain thought Bowman was merely offering his congratulations for the third Stanley Cup they have won together. But then Bowman leaned over and told him he had just coached his last game.

"My first reaction was probably shock," Yzerman said. "And then just as quickly I

THE FINALS

JULIAN H. GONZALEZ

Scotty Bowman and wife Suella prepared to leave Joe Louis Arena after Scotty's final game as coach.

found myself to be very happy. Happy for him because he's leaving on his own terms, having won the Stanley Cup in his last game. How can you have a better ending than that?

"Without him," Yzerman said, pointing to the red-and-white confetti on the ice, "none of this was possible. He taught me how to win. He taught us all that the only thing that matters is getting to this point where the only goal, the only objective that you consider accept-

able, is winning the Stanley Cup."

Bowman's wife, Suella, knew soon after the Olympics that he wasn't coming back, but she was sworn to secrecy. She was under the impression that he wouldn't announce his plans until the parades and platitudes were finished in a few days.

"But I get down to the ice and I find out that Scott had already told everyone," she said. "So when I find him I ask him if I can finally answer questions now about this,

and he said it was fine. I'm very happy for Scott, but I'm even happier for us and our family because now we'll have more time together to explore more things in life."

"It's not that I no longer enjoy coaching because I do," Bowman said. "I just thought that this was the right time to do this. I've had a great time in Detroit. The Ilitches have been wonderful people to work for, and this is a great, great hockey city. I just felt that it was time to move on."

Man of the hour

JULIAN H. GONZALEZ

Swedish defenseman Nicklas Lidstrom took a big gulp from the Stanley Cup after he became the first European to win the Conn Smythe Trophy as the playoff MVP.

BY HELENE ST. JAMES

Nicklas Lidstrom became the first European to win the Conn Smythe Trophy as the most valuable player in the playoffs.

"I think that makes it even sweeter, being the first European to win it," the Swede said after the Red Wings' Game 5 victory over Carolina clinched the Stanley Cup. "It's very nice. We had lots of leaders on the club, starting with Dom back in net. We had goal scorers that could have won it easily, so I am very proud, and it is a tremendous honor to win this award."

Other strong candidates were Dominik Hasek, Sergei Fedorov and the Captain, Steve Yzerman.

But none surpassed Lidstrom.

"Oh, was I happy," said associate coach Dave Lewis, who is in charge of the defense. "It's about time he got some recognition. What a player! He is probably, if not one of the best defensemen in hockey history, he is side-by-side with anybody."

Lidstrom played a tremendous role throughout the playoffs, highlighted by his monumental performance in Game 3 of the finals. As the game dragged on into the third overtime, Lidstrom was on the ice for 52:03, the only skater on either team to hit the 50-minute mark. Two nights earlier, he was on the ice for 34:38 in a regulation game.

"Look what Nick Lidstrom did

all the way through the playoffs, the minutes he logged," Scotty Bowman said. "He's just about a perfect player on the ice. Very few mistakes. He scored some big goals for us. It's a wonderful tribute to him."

Rarely did Lidstrom play less than 30 minutes. He was on the first power-play unit and often played the entire two minutes it takes to kill a penalty. If the Wings were desperate for a goal, they put him on the ice. And it often worked.

"He's been there for us every game — every shift he has played so great," Tomas Holmstrom said. "I'm glad he got it because he was the best defensive player all through the series."

What a wonderful world

BY MICHAEL ROSENBERG

And then it was over and the championship was won and the crowd slipped into delirium and "What a Night" blared on the loudspeakers and the Red Wings gathered near their own goal, mission accomplished.

And the Carolina Hurricanes waited, smile-less, and watched as the Wings celebrated.

And the esteemed Prof. Igor Larionov saw this, and he skated over to start the end-of-the-series handshake, and he was soon followed by Steve Yzerman and Brendan Shanahan and then the rest of the Wings.

And out walked NHL commissioner Gary Bettman, who was promptly booed, and then Bettman said a bunch of things that didn't need to be said, because that's what people do when they present trophies after sporting events.

And finally Bettman handed the Conn Smythe Trophy to Nicklas Lidstrom, the playoff MVP, and Lidstrom smiled, perhaps because Bettman didn't ask him to give a speech.

And Section 203 chanted, "We want the Cup! We want the Cup!" and soon the whole arena joined in.

And then came the Cup.

And Bettman presented it to Steve Yzerman, who immediately called for Scotty Bowman, and the crowd went nuts, unaware that Bowman had just coached his last game.

And Bowman, who knows the Stanley Cup so well he calls it Stan, skated with the Cup that he had just won for a record ninth time.

And then Bowman handed the Cup back to Yzerman, who called for Dominik Hasek, and the goalie skated with the Cup for the first time.

And then the Cup went to Luc

JULIAN H. GONZALEZ

Brett Hull skated with the trophy for a second time, first time as a Red Wing. He had helped the Dallas Stars win it in 1999.

Robitaille, who had temporarily moved away from his family in Los Angeles for a chance for this moment, and Robitaille's family watched from nearby as Robitaille skated with the Cup.

And then it went to other first-time winners — to Steve Du-

chesne and then to Fredrik Olausson, the understated Swede, who skated in a brief circle before handing the Cup to Chris Chelios.

And then Chelios, who had won the Cup in 1986 with Montreal — with Patrick Roy as his goalie — handed the Cup to Jiri Slegr.

KIRTHMON F. DOZIER

And Slegr, a replacement for the suspended Jiri Fischer, handed the Cup to Fischer.

And "What a Wonderful World" came over the loudspeakers, and as Louis Armstrong sang, "I hear babies crying; I watch them grow; they'll learn much more than I'll ever know," the Wings' children wandered around the ice, into the dream.

And then the Cup went to another first-time winner, Boyd Devereaux, who handed it to Mathieu Dandenault, who handed it to Pavel Datsyuk, the brilliant young Russian.

And Datsyuk handed it to first-time winner Manny Legace, who handed it to another first-time winner, Jason Williams, and Williams handed it to Lidstrom.

And then it went to Shanahan, who had struggled so mightily in these playoffs before scoring three goals in the final two games.

And then it went to Brett Hull, the final major free-agent signee from last summer.

And then to the Grind Line, Kris Draper and Darren McCarty and Kirk Maltby, who did so much more than grind in these playoffs.

And then to Larionov, the oldest player in the league, and Tomas Holmstrom, one of the toughest.

And then to Sergei Fedorov, and as he so often does, Fedorov skated faster and farther than everybody else.

And then "Bad to the Bone" played, apparently because they ran out of music.

But what they must have thought to themselves, as they gathered for the team photo, piled around the only trophy that keeps them up at night, with Bowman sprawled in front like a little kid and family members jumping into the camera frame, what they must have thought to themselves was, oh, what a wonderful world.

On the biggest day of the year for Wings fans, the Stanley Cup arrived in Windsor by train from Toronto. Phil Pritchard, the keeper of the Cup, then drove it over to the Joe.

J. KYLE KEENER

They came by land and they came by river to salute the heroes of Hockeytown.

RICHARD LEE

Happy fans took to the streets of Royal Oak after the Wings wrapped up the Cup with a 3-1 victory.

Outside Joe
Louis Arena,
the women
who called
themselves
the Fine Line —
from left,
Kristin
Wiseman,
Rose Peruski,
Kelli Williams
and Amy
Wiseman —
waited
for players
to arrive
before the
decisive
Game 5.

MANDI WRIGHT

J. KYLE KEENER

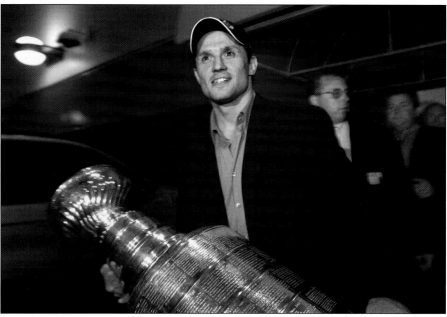

Oh, yeah.
Nothing could
be finer —
good-bye,
Carolina.
When it
was over,
the Captain
and his Cup
headed
for home.

MANDI WRIGHT

Cup finals summaries

GAME 1
HURRICANES 3, WINGS 2 (OT)

Carolina	0	2	0	1—3
Detroit	1	1	0	0—2

First period
Detroit, Fedorov 5 (Yzerman), 15:21 (pp).

Second period
Carolina, Hill 4 (Kapanen, Francis), 3:30 (pp).
Detroit, Maltby 2 (McCarty), 10:39.
Carolina, O'Neill 6 (Ward), 19:10.

Overtime
Carolina, Francis 6 (O'Neill, Kapanen), :58.

Penalties
1st: Hedican, Car (high-sticking), 8:03; Robitaille, Det (tripping), 10:28; Hill, Car (tripping), 11:15; Wesley, Car (interference), 14:45.
2nd: Carolina bench, served by Cole (too many men), :34; Larionov, Det (high-sticking), 2:07; Draper, Det (hooking), 2:44; Svoboda, Car (high-sticking), 4:28; Wallin, Car (roughing), 7:41; Dandenault, Det (tripping), 12:12.
3rd: Devereaux, Det (holding stick), 5:49; Larionov, Det (high-sticking), 12:17; Cole, Car (hooking), 18:19.

Shots: Carolina 7-13-5-1—26; Detroit 8-12-5-0—25. **Power plays:** Carolina 1 of 6; Detroit 1 of 7.
Goalies: Carolina, Irbe (10-4); Detroit, Hasek (12-7). **A:** 20,058.
Referees: Bill McCreary, Stephen Walkom. **Linesmen:** Brad Lazarowich, Brian Murphy.

SOME CAROLINA FANS DROVE UP FOR THE GAME, I SEE ...

MIKE THOMPSON

GAME 2
WINGS 3, HURRICANES 1

Carolina	1	0	0—1
Detroit	1	0	2—3

First period
Detroit, Maltby 3 (Draper, Chelios), 6:33 (sh).
Carolina, Brind'Amour 4, 14:47 (sh).

Third period
Detroit, Lidstrom 5 (Fedorov, Yzerman), 14:52 (pp).
Detroit, Draper 2 (Lidstrom, Olausson), 15:05.

Penalties
1st: Draper, Det (boarding), 1:25; Duchesne, Det (holding), 5:21; Hill, Car (slashing), 6:33; Svoboda, Car (roughing), 14:03; Hill, Car (holding), 16:23. **2nd:** Battaglia, Car (holding), 1:05; Duchesne, Det (tripping), 3:55; Detroit bench, served by Devereaux (too many men), 7:23; Gelinas, Car (interference), 10:10; Ward, Car (holding), 18:03. **3rd:** Fischer, Det (high-sticking), 9:38; Gelinas, Car (slashing), 14:00; Fischer, Det (slashing), 17:15; Battaglia, Car (charging), 17:45; Brind'Amour, Car (roughing), 19:33; Cole, Car (roughing), 19:33; Maltby, Det (roughing), 19:33; Chelios, Det (roughing), 19:33; McCarty, Det (roughing), 19:33; Hull, Det (tripping), 19:41.

Shots: Carolina 7-4-6—17. Detroit 9-8-13—30. **Power plays:** Carolina 0 of 8; Detroit 1 of 8. **Goalies:** Carolina, Irbe (10-5). Detroit, Hasek (13-7). **A:** 20,058. **Referees:** Paul Devorski, Don Koharski. **Linesmen:** Brad Lazarowich, Jean Morin.

GAME 3
WINGS 3, HURRICANES 2 (3 OT)

Detroit	0	1	1	0	0	1—3
Carolina	1	0	1	0	0	0—2

First period
Carolina, Vasicek 3 (Gelinas, Wesley), 14:49.

Second period
Detroit, Larionov 3 (Hull), 5:33.

Third period
Carolina, O'Neill 7 (Francis), 7:34.
Detroit, Hull 9 (Lidstrom, Fedorov), 18:46.

Third overtime
Detroit, Larionov 4 (Holmstrom, Duchesne), 14:47.

Penalties
1st: Brind'Amour, Car (holding stick), 1:45; Hedican, Car (boarding), 3:32; O'Neill, Car (boarding), 11:34; Lidstrom, Det (tripping), 12:30; Devereaux, Det (slashing), 19:15.
2nd: Maltby, Det (unsportsmanlike conduct), 5:13; Ward, Car (unsportsmanlike conduct), 5:13; Chelios, Det (interference), 8:12; Fedorov, Det (holding), 19:44; Hill, Car (holding), 19:44. **3rd:** Vasicek, Car (roughing), 5:25; Shanahan, Det (roughing), 5:25; Duchesne, Det (holding), 9:58; Hill, Car (roughing), 19:01; Shanahan, Det (roughing), 19:01. **1st OT:** Duchesne, Det (roughing), 18:23; Svoboda, Car (roughing), 18:23. **2nd OT:** Cole, Car (holding stick), 8:35; Olausson, Det (holding), 13:25.

Shots: Detroit 6-7-16-11-6-7—53; Carolina 8-6-7-5-8-9—43. **Power plays:** Detroit 0 of 4; Carolina 0 of 5.

MIKE THOMPSON

Goalies: Detroit, Hasek (14-7); Carolina, Irbe (10-6). **A:** 18,982. **Referees:** Bill McCreary, Stephen Walkom. **Linesmen:** Brian Murphy, Dan Schachte.

GAME 4
WINGS 3, HURRICANES 0

Detroit	0	1	2—3
Carolina	0	0	0—0

Second period
Detroit, Hull 10 (Devereaux, Olausson), 6:32.

Third period
Detroit, Larionov 5 (Fischer, Robitaille), 3:43.

Detroit, Shanahan 6 (Fedorov, Chelios), 14:43.

Penalties
1st: Wesley, Car (hooking), 2:05; Cole, Car (goalie interference), 16:54; Fedorov, Det (high-sticking), 16:54. **2nd:** Robitaille, Det (high-sticking), 9:06; Duchesne, Det (holding stick), 14:34. **3rd:** Hill, Car (boarding), 8:34. **Shots:** Detroit 10-6-11—27. Carolina 6-7-4—17. **Power plays:** Detroit 0 of 2; Carolina 0 of 2. **Goalies:** Detroit, Hasek (15-7). Carolina, Irbe (10-7). **A:** 18,986. **Referees:** Paul Devorski, Don Koharski. **Linesmen:** Jean Morin, Dan Schachte.

GAME 5
WINGS 3, HURRICANES 1

Carolina	0	1	0—1
Detroit	0	2	1—3

Second period
Detroit, Holmstrom 8 (Larionov, Chelios), 4:07.
Detroit, Shanahan 7 (Fedorov, Yzerman), 14:04 (pp).
Carolina, O'Neill 8 (Hill, Wesley), 18:50 (pp).

Third period
Detroit, Shanahan 8 (Yzerman), 19:15 (en).

Penalties
1st: Carolina bench, served by Vasicek (too many men), 12:09. **2nd:** Slegr, Det (holding), 6:00; Svoboda, Car (roughing), 13:34; Cole, Car (roughing), 16:15; Shanahan, Det (hooking), 16:53. **3rd:** Fedorov, Det (cross-checking), 5:23; Vasicek, Car (interference), 8:12.

Shots: Carolina 5-7-5—17. Detroit 12-8-7—27. **Power play:** Carolina 1 of 3; Detroit 1 of 4. **Goalies:** Carolina, Irbe (10-8). Detroit, Hasek (16-7). **A:** 20,058. **Referees:** Bill McCreary, Stephen Walkom. **Linesmen:** Brad Lazarowich, Brian Murphy.

The players

The 2001-2002 Red Wings (with regular-season and playoff statistics):

SEAN AVERY
No. 42; C, 5-10, 185; age 22

The Hockeytown hearthrob didn't play in the playoffs after appearing in 36 regular-season games.

GP	G	A	PTS	+/-	PM
36	2	2	4	+1	68
—	—	—	—	—	—

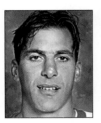

CHRIS CHELIOS
No. 24; D, 6-1, 190; age 40

After leading the league with a plus-minus rating that matched his age, he kept on going. He led the team in the playoffs at plus-15. Chelios also battled the likes of Todd Bertuzzi, Keith Tkachuk and Peter Forsberg.

GP	G	A	PTS	+/-	PM
79	6	33	39	+40	126
23	1	13	14	+15	44

MATHIEU DANDENAULT
No. 11; D, 6-1, 200; age 26

After playing relatively well in the top four much of the regular season, he played well with Steve Duchesne in the third pair. He used his speed as an asset, pinching effectively when needed. After getting two Cup rings without playing in the finals, he had plenty of ice time against Carolina on the way to earning his third.

GP	G	A	PTS	+/-	PM
81	8	12	20	-5	44
23	1	2	3	+7	8

PAVEL DATSYUK
No. 13; C, 5-11, 180; age 23

The rookie had a rough introduction to playoff hockey. But after sitting out a couple of games in the first round, he came on strong, showing the same dazzling puckhandling ability he did during the regular season.

GP	G	A	PTS	+/-	PM
70	11	24	35	+4	4
21	3	3	6	+1	2

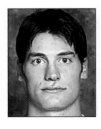

BOYD DEVEREAUX
No. 21; F, 6-2, 195; age 24

After sitting out the first two playoff games, both losses, he returned to the lineup and didn't come out. Digging out pucks for Pavel Datsyuk and Brett Hull, he didn't look like he had played only three playoff games before this season.

GP	G	A	PTS	+/-	PM
79	9	16	25	+9	24
21	2	4	6	+5	4

KRIS DRAPER
No. 33; F, 5-11, 190; age 31

After playing right wing on a scoring line much of the regular season, he returned to centering the Grind Line and doing his usual dirty work. He was an effective penalty killer, and sealed the Game 2 victory over Carolina with a late goal.

GP	G	A	PTS	+/-	PM
82	15	15	30	+26	56
23	2	3	5	+4	20

STEVE DUCHESNE
No. 28; D, 6-0, 195; age 36

Soft? Did somebody call him soft? OK, he's not a prototypical, physical, playoff-type defenseman. But in advancing past the second round for the first time, he was hungry enough to do anything for his first Cup. He hit. He moved the puck well.

GP	G	A	PTS	+/-	PM
64	3	15	18	+3	28
23	0	6	6	+6	24

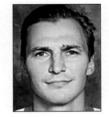

SERGEI FEDOROV
No. 91; C, 6-2, 200; age 32

He didn't score as often as he would have liked. But he has been a brilliant two-way player, taking extra shifts, averaging more ice time than any other Detroit forward. Igor Larionov said Fedorov played his best hockey, and that was a huge compliment.

GP	G	A	PTS	+/-	PM
81	31	37	68	+20	36
23	5	14	19	+4	20

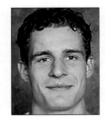

JIRI FISCHER
No. 2; D, 6-5, 210; age 21

He came along well this season and has come along well in the playoffs, having entered with only five games' experience. He played hurt early. He was suspended for the final game after cross-checking Carolina's Tommy Westlund in Game 4.

GP	G	A	PTS	+/-	PM
80	2	8	10	+17	67
22	3	3	6	+6	30

DOMINIK HASEK
No. 39; G, 6-2, 170; age 37

When the Wings were trailing Colorado, 3-2, we said he had to come up big, and he did. His six playoff shutouts set an NHL record. He won his first Cup — what he came here for and why the Wings acquired him.

GP	AVG	W-L-T	SO	GA
65	2.17	41-15-8	5	140
23	1.86	16-7-0	6	45

TOMAS HOLMSTROM
No. 96; F, 6-0, 210; age 29

After scoring only eight goals during the regular season, he scored eight in the playoffs, including the Wings' first in the final game against Carolina. After rating minus-12 during the regular season, he was plus-7. Enough said.

GP	G	A	PTS	+/-	PM
69	8	18	26	-12	58
23	8	3	11	+7	8

BRETT HULL
No. 17; F, 5-11, 205; age 37

Although he showed he is a complete player, he was brought in to score. And he did. He had his droughts, but he led the team with 10 playoff goals.

GP	G	A	PTS	+/-	PM
82	30	33	63	+18	35
23	10	8	18	+1	4

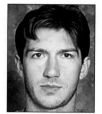

MAXIM KUZNETSOV
No. 32; D, 6-6, 235; age 25

He continued to develop during the regular season, but didn't play in the postseason.

GP	G	A	PTS	+/-	PM
39	1	2	3	E	40
—	—	—	—	—	—

IGOR LARIONOV
No. 8; C, 5-11, 170; age 41

He suffered a sprained knee in the St. Louis series and didn't look good when he returned. But otherwise, the professorial playmaker looked fresh, particularly when he scored the winner in triple overtime of Game 3 against Carolina.

GP	G	A	PTS	+/-	PM
70	11	32	43	-5	50
18	5	6	11	+5	4

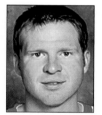

MANNY LEGACE
No. 34; G, 5-9, 162; age 29

He didn't play much in the postseason, but he was a solid backup to Dominik Hasek.

GP	AVG	W-L-T	SO	GA
20	2.42	10-6-2	1	45
1	5.45	0-0-0	0	1

NICKLAS LIDSTROM
No. 5; D, 6-2, 190; age 32

The Norris Trophy finalist added the Conn Smythe Trophy to his collection by being his usual, dependable, quiet self, logging the most minutes among Detroit skaters and doing it against top players. He scored the winning goal in Game 2 against Carolina.

GP	G	A	PTS	+/-	PM
78	9	50	59	+13	20
23	5	11	16	+6	2

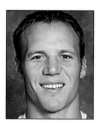

KIRK MALTBY
No. 18; F, 6-0, 185; age 29

The crowd chanted his last name as the Wings chased away the Blues in the second round, because he put his body in front of shots.

GP	G	A	PTS	+/-	PM
82	9	15	24	+15	40
23	3	3	6	+7	32

DARREN McCARTY
No. 25; F, 6-1, 215; age 30

He scored five goals during the regular season. He scored none in the first two rounds. Then he scored four on Patrick Roy.

GP	G	A	PTS	+/-	PM
62	5	7	12	+2	98
23	4	4	8	+5	34

FREDRIK OLAUSSON
No. 27; D, 6-0, 195; age 35

He did more than score that overtime goal in Game 3 against Colorado. After falling out of favor in the second half of the regular season, he rejoined the lineup in Game 3 of the Vancouver series and played well with Nicklas Lidstrom. He improved as the playoffs progressed.

GP	G	A	PTS	+/-	PM
47	2	13	15	+9	22
21	2	4	6	+3	10

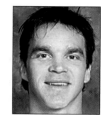

LUC ROBITAILLE
No. 20; F, 6-1, 215; age 36

He sacrificed ice time or didn't earn it, depending on your perspective. Of his four goals, two were lucky. But, hey, that's why he's "Lucky Luc." Regardless, he finally got his name on the Cup, which is why he came to Detroit.

GP	G	A	PTS	+/-	PM
81	30	20	50	-2	38
23	4	5	9	+4	10

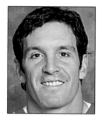

BRENDAN SHANAHAN
No. 14; F, 6-3, 220; age 33

He had a great regular season, and his winning goal and the ensuing empty-netter in Game 5 against Carolina made up for a lot of bad luck in the playoffs. He finished tied for second on the team, with 19 points.

GP	G	A	PTS	+/-	PM
80	37	38	75	+23	118
23	8	11	19	+5	20

JIRI SLEGR
No. 71; D, 6-0, 220; age 31

The trade-deadline acquisition from Atlanta didn't play until the final game against Carolina, when he filled in for the suspended Jiri Fischer.

GP	G	A	PTS	+/-	PM
46	3	6	9	-20	59
1	0	0	0	+2	2

JASON WILLIAMS
No. 29; F, 5-11, 185; age 21

The rookie was hot at the end of the regular season, scoring four goals in his final three games. When he played, he played well. He was on the top line with Shanahan and Steve Yzerman for a game against Colorado.

GP	G	A	PTS	+/-	PM
25	8	2	10	+2	4
9	0	0	0	-1	2

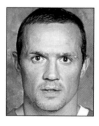

STEVE YZERMAN
No. 19; C, 5-11, 185; age 37

Grinding on his bum right knee, he led the team with 23 points. He scored big goals. He showed his legendary leadership qualities. Who knows where the Wings would have been without him?

GP	G	A	PTS	+/-	PM
52	13	35	48	+11	18
23	6	17	23	+4	10

Four newspaper sports front pages displayed on the page.

FRIDAY
April 26, 2002

SPORTS
THE FREE PRESS

Section D

COUNTDOWN
13
Victories needed to capture the Wings' 10th Stanley Cup.

DETROIT 4, VANCOUVER 0
STANLEY CUP PLAYOFFS

Dominators

The Joe Louis crowd mirrors Boyd Devereaux after he scores the third goal of the Red Wings' four-goal outburst in the first period Thursday night.

DREW SHARP
Vancouver general manager's envy inflates spirit of Detroit

Hasek, Red Wings put on a show, take third straight from Canucks
By NICHOLAS J. COTSONIKA

INSIDE

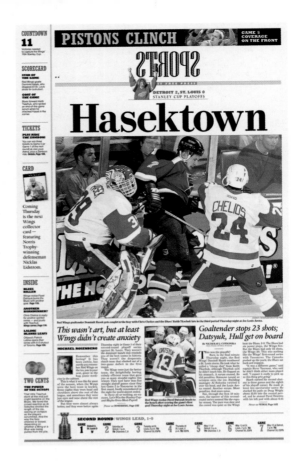

PISTONS CLINCH
GAME 5 COVERAGE ON THE FRONT

SPORTS
THE FREE PRESS

DETROIT 2, ST. LOUIS 0
STANLEY CUP PLAYOFFS

Hasektown

Red Wings goaltender Dominik Hasek gets caught in the fray with Chris Chelios and the Blues' Keith Tkachuk late in the third period Thursday night at Joe Louis Arena.

This wasn't art, but at least Wings didn't create anxiety
MICHAEL ROSENBERG

Goaltender stops 23 shots; Datsyuk, Hull get on board
By NICHOLAS J. COTSONIKA

NBA | NETS ADVANCE; LAKERS SURVIVE
New Jersey knocks out Boston, 96-88, and the Lakers beat the Kings, 106-102. PAGE 6B.

WORLD CUP SOCCER
World Cup coverage on www.freep.com.

SATURDAY
June 1, 2002

SPORTS
THE FREE PRESS

Section B

COUNTDOWN
4
Victories needed to capture the Wings' 10th Stanley Cup.

DETROIT 7, COLORADO 0
STANLEY CUP PLAYOFFS

Au Rev-Roy!

THE MAGNIFICENT SEVEN

Red Wings exercise demons by pummeling nemesis Roy
DREW SHARP

And bring on Carolina as blowout sends Wings to final
By NICHOLAS J. COTSONIKA

U.S. thwarts dirty-bomb plot tied to Al Qaeda. PAGE 1A

REGULAR FREE PRESS INSIDE

STANLEY CUP FINALS

METRO FINAL
50 cents

Detroit Free Press
www.freep.com

TUESDAY
June 11, 2002

HULL-ACIOUS!
Brett's 100th wins it; Cup is 1 victory away

GAME 4
DET 3
CAR 0

These numbers tell the story for the Wings
MITCH ALBOM

Red Wings' Brett Hull, left, and Boyd Devereaux celebrate Hull's second-period goal Monday night.

KNIGHT RIDDER